AF249119

Prelude to the Modernist Crisis

AMERICAN ACADEMY OF RELIGION

RELIGION IN TRANSLATION

HERMENEUTICS
The Handwritten Manuscripts

Friedrich D. E. Schleiermacher
Edited by Heina Kimmerle
Translated by James Duke and Jack Forstman

THE STUDY OF STOLEN LOVE
Translated by David C. Buck and K. Paramasivam

THE DAOIST MONASTIC MANUAL
A Translation of the *Fengdao Kejie*
Livia Kohn

SACRED AND PROFANE BEAUTY
The Holy in Art

Garardus van der Leeuw
Preface by Mircea Eliade
Translated by David E. Green
With a New Introduction and Bibliography by Diane
Apostolos-Cappadona

THE HISTORY OF THE BUDDHA'S RELIC SHRINE
A Translation of the Sinhala Thūpavamsa

Stephen C. Berkwitz

DAMASCIUS' *PROBLEMS AND SOLUTIONS CONCERNING
FIRST PRINCIPLES*

Translated by Sara Ahbel-Rappe
Introduction and Notes by Sara Ahbel-Rappe

THE SECRET GARLAND
Antal's Tiruppavai and Nacciyar Tirumoli

Translated with Introduction and Commentary by Archana Venkatesan

PRELUDE TO THE MODERNIST CRISIS
The "Firmin" Articles of Alfred Loisy

Edited by C. J. T. Talar
Translated by Christine E. Thirlway

Prelude to the Modernist Crisis

The "Firmin" Articles of Alfred Loisy

TRANSLATED BY CHRISTINE E. THIRLWAY

EDITED, WITH AN INTRODUCTION,

BY C. J. T. TALAR

UNIVERSITY PRESS

2010

# OXFORD
UNIVERSITY PRESS

Oxford University Press, Inc., publishes works that further
Oxford University's objective of excellence
in research, scholarship, and education.

Oxford   New York
Auckland   Cape Town   Dar es Salaam   Hong Kong   Karachi
Kuala Lumpur   Madrid   Melbourne   Mexico City   Nairobi
New Delhi   Shanghai   Taipei   Toronto

With offices in
Argentina   Austria   Brazil   Chile   Czech Republic   France   Greece
Guatemala   Hungary   Italy   Japan   Poland   Portugal   Singapore
South Korea   Switzerland   Thailand   Turkey   Ukraine   Vietnam

Published by Oxford University Press, Inc.
198 Madison Avenue, New York, New York 10016
www.oup.com

Oxford is a registered trademark of Oxford University Press

Library of Congress Cataloging-in-Publication Data
Loisy, Alfred, 1857–1940.
[Selections. English. 2010]
Prelude to the modernist crisis : the Firmin articles of Alfred Loisy / translated by
Christine E. Thirlway ; edited, with an introduction, by C. J. T. Talar.
p. cm. — (AAR religion in translation)
ISBN 978-0-19-975457-1
1. Modernism (Christian theology)—Catholic Church.
I. Talar, C. J. T., 1947–   II. Title.
BX1396.L6513 2010
230'.2 — dc22   2010001089

9 8 7 6 5 4 3 2 1

Printed in the United States of America
on acid-free paper

Contents

Introduction   vii
C. J. T. Talar

The "Firmin" Articles
Alfred Loisy
Translated by Christine E. Thirlway

The Development of Christianity According
to Cardinal Newman   3

The Individualist Theory of Religion   17

The Definition of Religion   31

The Idea of Revelation   45

The Proofs and the Economy of Revelation   63

New Theology   87
Charles Maignen
Translated by Christine E. Thirlway

Notes   101
Index   107

Introduction

C.J.T. Talar

To be at all familiar with Roman Catholic modernism is to have at least some acquaintance with Alfred Firmin Loisy (1857–1940), whose *L'Évangile et l'Église* (1902) may be said to have precipitated the modernist crisis. Under the guise of a critique of the liberal Protestant theologian Adolf von Harnack,[1] Loisy sought to highlight the shortcomings of the neo-scholasticism reigning in Catholic theology and to suggest the contours of an alternative apologetic better adapted to minds formed by modernity. The historical treatment of these issues in *L'Évangile et l'Église* had been preceded by a series of articles published in the *Revue du clergé français* between 1898 and 1900 under the pseudonym "A. Firmin": "Le développement chrétien d'après le cardinal Newman" (vol. 17 [1898]: 5–20); "La théorie individualiste de la religion" (vol. 17 [1899]: 202–15); "La définition de la religion" (vol. 18 [1899]: 193–209); "L'idée de la revelation" (vol. 21 [1900]: 250–71); "Les preuves et l'économie de la revelation" (vol. 22 [1900]: 126–53); and "La religion d'Israël" (vol. 24 [1900]: 337–63). They formed the theoretical background to the historical apologetic set forth in the book. Lacking acquaintance with those articles, many of the book's initial readers seriously misunderstood it.[2] Given the voluminous literature on Loisy that has appeared since, present-day readers are less likely to go astray, but the fact remains that Loisy composed the work with great subtlety and a degree of ambiguity. In Gabriel Daly's characterization, *L'Évangile et l'Église* "still fascinates both by the elegance of its style and by a dexterity which verges on sleight-of-hand."[3] While the book has long been available in English,[4] the Firmin articles that constitute its basis and clarify its positions remained untranslated. The present work provides a translation of the first five of those articles. The sixth, on the religion of Israel, originally was to appear in three parts. However, after the first installment appeared in the *Revue*, the archbishop of Paris, Cardinal Richard,[5] issued a condemnation of it, and Loisy's collaboration with the *Revue* ceased. Loisy published the complete text in 1901 as *La religion d'Israël*, in an edition for private circulation. An expanded version went on sale in 1908, which formed the basis for an English translation of 1910.[6] Thus, it was not thought necessary to include a translation of the last Firmin article here. A response to the first of the articles by Charles Maignen[7] does find a place, however. It gives an indication of a line of criticism of Loisy's work prior to *L'Évangile et l'Église*, from a critic who would return to the lists to engage the latter,[8] as well as its sequel, *Autour d'un petit livre* (1903).[9]

In what follows, the Firmin articles will be situated in the context of Loisy's career.[10] Then their content will be examined briefly to highlight issues that became volatile at the time of the modernist crisis. Finally, Maignen's criticism will be touched upon, to indicate the tenor of a type of reaction to this developing apologetic.

The Context

Ernest Renan died on October 2, 1892.[11] Catholic critics were not slow to mark his passing, in the main with legible sighs of relief, given this apostate's role in placing the results of biblical criticism before the wider public.[12] In the course of a not uncritical, but also not unsympathetic, article on Renan, which appeared later that same month, Mgr Maurice d'Hulst[13] conjectured what the outcome might have been if Renan's education had been conducted along the lines of the instruction given at the Institut catholique de Paris in the 1890s rather than that received at the seminary of Saint-Sulpice in the 1840s. The apologetics then served up to Renan was not proof against his independent reading of German philosophy, his mastery of Hebrew, and exposure to German rationalist criticism. Having lost his faith, he left the seminary in October 1845 and embarked upon an academic career that would include a professorship at the Collège de France (where Loisy would later follow his lectures) and election to the Académie française. While admitting the precarious nature of what-might-have-beens, d'Hulst wondered if Renan's life would have followed a different path "had he been exposed to what our independent faculties of theology today offer to clerics…an instruction more sound, views less timid, principles less narrow, and responses better adapted to new difficulties?"[14] In the early 1890s, then, the jury was still out—at least in moderately progressive circles—regarding the use of critical methods by Catholic scholars who had benefited from the intellectual renewal that was taking place in French Catholicism in the last quarter of the nineteenth century. A decade later, evidence was amassing toward a decidedly unfavorable verdict. In November 1902, coinciding with the appearance of *L'Évangile et l'Église*, the Dominican exegete Marie-Joseph Lagrange[15] gave a series of lectures at the Institut catholique de Toulouse on the subject of historical-critical method. Their subsequent publication, in March 1903, as *La méthode historique, surtout à propos de l'Ancien Testament*, was viewed from some quarters as indicative of collusion among partisans of theological innovation, not mere coincidence.[16] Suspicions regarding the implications of Loisy's work apparently found confirmation in the clarifications of *Autour d'un petit livre*. The verdict became official with the condemnation of five of Loisy's books by the Holy Office in December 1903.[17] By 1904 Loisy's active participation in the modernist movement had ceased, although his excommunication would not come until 1908.

The decade between the publication of d'Hulst's article on Renan and *L'Évangile et l'Église* is thus crucial for understanding the genesis and reception of the Firmin articles. However, since Loisy's apologetical ambitions well antedate the 1890s, it will be necessary to retrieve earlier portions of his career. While interpretation of Loisy's theological development remains controverted,[18] the basic events of his career are clear enough and may be rehearsed briefly here.

A combination of frail health and intellectual achievement oriented Loisy toward a life of study. In his autobiographical *Choses passées*, he describes the promptings that led him toward priesthood. The program of studies he encountered in seminary, based on manuals that were intended to support less gifted students and discourage creativity on the part of more gifted instructors, provided little in the way of challenge to Loisy. In search of more substantial fare, he sought to supplement the seminary textbooks with the *Summa Theologiae* of Saint Thomas Aquinas. However, such independent labors served only to deepen his dissatisfaction with theology. Initially through another student, then continuing on his own, he learned Hebrew—to better effect. The availability of a small library, a legacy to the seminary, enabled him to practice some rudimentary textual criticism. Forced to find his way on his own, he did not, as he later admitted, advance far enough to make any troubling discoveries.[19]

While Loisy was in the midst of these studies, a law was passed that would profoundly affect the course of his future. In 1875 French Catholics obtained the right to open universities empowered to grant degrees. The bishops were quick to seize the opportunity before political fortunes changed, and Catholic universities were shortly established at Paris, Angers, Lyon, Lille, and, somewhat later, Toulouse.[20] By March 1876 faculties of arts, sciences, and law had been set up at Paris. At Rome's insistence, the École supérieure de théologie was added to them in 1878. Loisy was designated by his bishop to become a member of its first class. What he found there was, in the main, hardly the stuff of intellectual liberation.[21] In any case, his initial sojourn was short-lived. His health broke down, and the new year found him back in his diocese, where he received diaconate in March and ordination to priesthood that June. Assignment to a rural parish left him ample leisure to continue his independent study, and it was at this point that he "undertook for the first time an exposition of Catholic doctrine geared to the needs of modern times."[22] He soon abandoned the project, realizing that he lacked sufficient background to do it justice. Still, it serves to indicate the shape of things to come. As Loisy later remarked, "From the same preoccupation will issue, twenty years later, those of my writings which have been branded modernist."[23]

After two years of parish ministry, Loisy succeeded in gaining reappointment to Paris, to the recently renamed Institut catholique. The level of instruction there had not, for the most part, undergone much improvement during his absence, although he manifests greater appreciation for the church historian Louis Duchesne's work.[24] Duchesne had imported into the Institut the research orientation and practices he had imbibed at the École pratique des hautes études. But Loisy's direct contact with these via his studies in Assyriology at the École, and with Renan's lectures at the Collège de France, proved to be more decisive. Loisy credits Renan with providing him "the model of an excellent method" of textual criticism, which contrasted with the haphazard and trial-and-error nature of his self-guided efforts.[25] It also contrasts with the approach characteristic of Catholic biblical manuals.[26]

While opportunities external to the Institut were important, those internal were no less so. Loisy may have been less than impressed by the instruction he received there, but through a combination of circumstances he himself was soon placed in a position to teach. In 1881 Loisy's largely self-acquired proficiency in Hebrew enabled him to assume responsibility for that course. (It also provided a catalyst for his following Renan's lectures on the subject, from 1882 to 1885.) In 1886, as a result of his work at the École pratique, he added Assyrian to the instruction in Hebrew, and by the end of the 1880s had also been given a significant share in the course on scripture.[27] Loisy came to view the formation of ecclesiastical students as crucial in contributing to a climate receptive to critical work and a future source of support in its favor. He sought to extend his influence beyond the classroom by publishing his lectures and his independent research.[28]

As a movement for renewal within Catholicism, modernism stands within a liberal tradition that, throughout the nineteenth century, attempted to adapt the church's theology, practice, and institutional structures to modernity. Modernism's distinguishing characteristics reside in the terms under which this attempted adaptation was carried out. It was catalyzed by the felt need to come to terms with the emerging religious sciences which extended their positive methods to sacred texts heretofore considered sacrosanct. This project posed some serious problems:

> Initiation into these methods posed a disturbing dilemma to the Catholic scholar: to see in this scientific laicization of the religious universe an intrinsic contradiction and a culpable profanation was to renounce all serious work and assume a position of inferiority; while to accept the rules seemed to introduce unrestricted investigation into a religion which excluded that and, more precisely, to vastly multiply difficulties refractory to any apologetic or authoritative treatment.[29]

Loisy's initial attempt at a renewal of apologetics, noted earlier, drew inspiration from the liberal Catholicism of Henri Lacordaire (1802–61) and Charles de Montalembert (1810–70) to which he had been exposed in seminary. But he soon became aware that he lacked the background to carry out the project. His exposure to practitioners of religious sciences at the École pratique des hautes études and Collège de France tended to deepen his sense of the dilemma rather than show any clear way to solve it. Out of a sense of a need to proceed carefully in an ecclesiastical climate clearly suspicious of historical criticism, combined with a conviction that a way forward would emerge with time, Loisy evolved a strategy that would occupy his teaching with largely technical matters of exegesis. Areas such as inspiration and inerrancy, which had unavoidable theological implications, he would reserve for the future.[30] If, during the 1880s, his deepening knowledge of secular science brought home the radical nature of any projected renewal of traditional Catholicism,[31] and occasioned a retreat from theological and apologetic concerns to more technical matters of exegesis, by the early 1890s his contact with students rekindled his hopes that a means of conciliation between modernity and tradition could be negotiated.

Despite his caution, Loisy's work encountered opposition. In a climate in which the conservative biblical scholarship of Fulcran Vigouroux's

Manuel biblique could prove unsettling for some ecclesiastics, such opposition occasions little surprise. But when, gradualist strategies notwithstanding, Loisy did run afoul of church authorities, the catalyst came from an unexpected quarter: from a well-meaning advocate rather than an adversary. It took the form of d'Hulst's article "La question biblique" (1893), which set in motion a series of events that led to Loisy's dismissal from his position at the Institut catholique.[32] The exegete used the controversy generated by the article as an occasion to set out rather clearly his own position on biblical inspiration and the related larger question of the connection between exegesis and theology. He advocated the independence of criticism from the outdated traditional notion of inspiration and from theological control more generally. As he later summed up his article, "Basically, it sanctioned the emancipation of scientific exegesis from dogma and theology, while at the same time it announced the formidable loss suffered by the traditionally received opinions as a result of critical work."[33]

Loisy's forced exit from the Institut catholique marked the end of his teaching career in Catholic higher education. It would have the unforeseen result of facilitating an alternative career in the secular university. It would also have an unforeseen impact on the nature of his published work. In being given a position as chaplain to a convent school in a Paris suburb, Loisy was largely deprived of the bibliographic resources to do serious exegetical work. At the same time, being obliged to give religious instruction motivated him to reflect on the presentation of Christian doctrine. This engaged him in apologetic issues and was reinforced by his contact with John Henry Newman's work. It bore fruit in a long apologetic work, *Essais d'histoire et de critique religieuses*, shortly revised and retitled *Essais d'histoire et de philosophie religieuses*.[34] From the work's first chapter, which examined four major current theories of religion—that of Roman Catholicism, as defined by the Vatican Council; Renan's rationalist conception; the liberal Protestant position, recently expressed by Auguste Sabatier; and the theory of Christian development proffered by Newman—Loisy extracted the first two Firmin articles on Newman and Sabatier, respectively. Its second chapter, entitled "Religion and Revelation," saw publication nearly integrally as the next three Firmin articles, taking up the definition of religion and aspects of revelation. Of the five historical chapters that followed, the first (chapter 3) saw partial publication in the *Revue du clergé français* as "La religion d'Israël" and was subsequently published integrally for private circulation. The four remaining from this section of the *Essais* were quarried for *L'Évangile et l'Église*, modified to accommodate the critique of Harnack and changes in Loisy's own position that had occurred in the interval. A final section, consisting of four additional chapters, returned to a more theoretical plane, privileging matters of reform over apologetics. A small amount of this material found its way into *Autour d'un petit livre*.[35] It is clear from the material in chapter 1 of the *Essais* omitted from publication in the *Revue du clergé français* that Loisy judged parts of his apologetic unacceptable to Catholicism in its current state. It is equally clear that he was optimistic enough regarding his chances for success to publish what he did, albeit in highly nuanced fashion. In a theory of development he apparently found a way forward through obstacles that had blocked his earlier attempts at formulating a reconciliation between Catholicism and modernity. Having suggested the significance of the Firmin articles for Loisy's own development, we may proceed to highlight themes prominent in them that were significant for the development of modernism.

The Content

Elsewhere I have suggested that modernism may usefully be conceptualized as a paradigm shift from a theology embedded in "classicist" culture to one reflective of "historical" culture.[36] This shift entailed a change in the conception of theology and its relation to its traditional conversation partners such as philosophy, history, and the natural sciences. It also involved an expansion in that conversation to include the emergent disciplines of history of religions and sociology. As a consequence, theology's problem set underwent modification, as well as methods deemed legitimate in solving those problems, and the data to be utilized in doing so. All of this sank deeper roots into an epistemological and metaphysical foundation that itself had shifted. Among other things, this meant that many of the basic notions of theology—revelation, dogma, miracle, prophecy, truth—were modified, not necessarily in their terminological expression but in their basic meaning. Part of the problem faced by theological innovators was that of expanding or modifying traditional notions to accommodate the results of secular science while demonstrating continuity between tradition and innovation. The Firmin articles show Loisy struggling to do justice to the "assured results of criticism" while avoiding the impression that he has preserved only the traditional vocabulary of Christianity with very little or nothing of its substance.

In *L'Évangile et l'Église* Loisy argued for the legitimacy and indeed inevitably of doctrinal development in Christianity. Countering the objection that the existence of this development was not recognized in a Catholicism that rejected the very notion of it, he wrote:

> Perhaps it would be nearer the truth to say that [the church] has never had consciousness of it, and she has no official theory concerning the philosophy of her own history. That which is taught by Vincent of Lérins, modern theologians (except Cardinal Newman) and the Council of the Vatican, touching the development of dogma, applies in reality to the definitely intellectual and theological phase of development, not to the first budding and formation of beliefs, or at least includes in an abstract definition, much work for which this definition is no adequate expression. It is just the idea of development which is now needed, not to be created all at once, but established from a better knowledge of the past.[37]

The notion of development, explicated through a network of organic metaphors (a trace of which is visible in the quoted extract), provided Loisy with the hermeneutical key he required. In focusing on change as a natural process of growth, he was able to admit very real historical differences in the church's teaching while preserving an element of continuity. In establishing a wide scope for development in Christianity's past, Loisy also made a case for significant development in the future. *L'Évangile et l'Église* remains rather vague about the forms any reforms of dogma, liturgy, or ecclesiastical structures may take, even in the immediate future. But it clearly seeks to establish a basis for revisionist hopes.

As the passage just quoted suggests, Loisy found John Henry Newman's work on the development of doctrine a useful legitimation for his own efforts, and this in more than one sense. In evoking Newman's name, he was obviously attempting to cover "the idea of development" with the mantle of the cardinalate. (It is no accident that some critics of Loisy's apologetic would relegate Newman's work in this case to his "Anglican period," detaching it from the "Catholic Newman" and delegitimating it thereby.) But, aside from Newman's ecclesiastical status, his work on development confirmed Loisy in a direction in which he was already moving when he encountered the cardinal's work in the 1890s. Newman accelerated Loisy's thought along lines it was already following, rather than constituting the original source of that thought.[38]

Given the role that development plays in *L'Évangile et l'Église*, it is less than surprising that Loisy passed over earlier sections of the initial chapter of the *Essais* and chose to begin the Firmin series with "Le développement chrétien d'après le cardinal Newman."[39] The first section of the article provides a competent summary of Newman's argument as set forth in the first edition of the *Essay on Development* (1845). Here Loisy is careful to link the conviction that change is fundamental to religious development with its necessity for all human development, on the one hand, and with the indispensability of an infallible authority, on the other. This juxtaposition of theological innovation with orthodox assertion is characteristic of the Firmin series more generally. Loisy then moves on in the second section to offer an evaluation of Newman's achievement. That "he has solved in principle all the difficulties which the theorists of individualist Christianity are at present raising against Catholic Christianity" (7–8)[40] both points ahead to subsequent articles in the series and suggests one of the factors that led to Newman being considered first. Likewise, the limitations in Newman's position that Loisy highlights also look ahead to a central concern: revelation. Examination of development must be extended to include scripture as well as the subsequent history of Christianity, and indeed must encompass the anterior religious history of humanity as well. This raises the question of how revelation enters into development, a question that "did not present itself to [Newman] in the terms in which it now presents itself to contemporary theology following the work of criticism done over the past fifty years" (10). This section ends on a note of praise for Newman's having perceived development as involving more than a matter of ideas and their codification into doctrines. Rather, it encompasses "the entire life of the Church." Loisy takes the occasion to note three "moments" of "every completed development" (11, 10). His relegation of the "dogmatic moment" to a tertiary position will lead to conflict with partisans of a dominant theology that accorded dogma pride of place.[41] The article's final portion surfaces objections to a theory of development and seeks to counter them. In a positive vein he argues for the theory's adequacy to "the legitimate conclusions of historical criticism" (16) and its superiority to understandings of Christianity set forth by prominent representatives of liberal Protestantism. Worth highlighting here is a statement culled from this closing section, as it strikes a "keynote" whose "echoes will be heard throughout the Firmin material, resounding against the walls of Liberal Protestantism and conservative Catholicism alike":[42]

> The development of Christianity cannot be reduced merely to
> a process of improving ecclesiastical language, a work of
> logical deduction or a multiplication of like practices,
> but...[such] development must be conceived as intimate, vital,
> real, as considerable in its order as that of animal life from
> birth to the adult state, implying, in consequence, the identity
> of the subject through all the transformations which take place
> in it according to the law of that institution, but excluding as a
> state of death, absolute immutability in the form once
> acquired. (14–15)

Loisy begins the second article of the Firmin series, "La théorie indi-vidualiste de la religion," with a reference to rationalism. But he quickly sets that aside (he will return to it in the second half of the next article, concerned with the definition of religion) to take up the two representatives of liberal Protestantism named at the close of "Le développement chrétien d'après le cardinal Newman": Adolf von Harnack and Auguste Sabatier.[43] Sabatier's work is accorded the greater prominence. In his handling of their approach to religion, Loisy is walking a thin line here. He later acknowledged that "the principal works out of which I was going to construct my apologetic synthesis [i.e., the *Essais*] were Harnack's *Dogmengeschichte*, whose first edition had appeared in 1885 and 1890, and Auguste Sabatier's *Esquisse d'un philosophie de la religion*, published very recently, in early 1897."[44] Yet if Loisy were perceived to adhere too closely to their positions, his revisionist apologetic would be labeled "liberal Protestant" and thereby effectively neutralized. While indebted to Harnack and Sabatier on some matters, he had to make a convincing differentiation of his stance from theirs. In seeking to accomplish this, Loisy will position them—Sabatier especially—as not so much wrong as partial and insufficient in their views. This will enable him to acknowledge points of solidarity, yet at the same time argue for the need for a decidedly Catholic corrective to compensate for their defects. Because polemical use is being made of both Sabatier and Harnack here, one should not expect to find a balanced presentation of their thought that does it full justice. Loisy's reading of liberal Protestantism remains rather selective, highlighting some aspects while leaving others in shadow, the better to establish his own position. This is not said to impugn Loisy's sincerity (as some critics have not hesitated to do) but to caution the reader that "Harnack" and "Sabatier" should continue to be mentally bracketed by quotation marks in the translations that follow.

The first of the three "moments" of development that surfaced in the initial Firmin article contains elements that connect it with the approach taken by liberal Protestantism. Before being the object of conceptual elaboration in theology, religion is rooted in human experience. In Sabatier's formulation, religion derives from the "feeling [*sentiment*] of powerlessness faced by 'universal determinism'" (20)—suggesting a dependence on Friedrich Schleiermacher (1768–1834), a dependence that Sabatier freely acknowledged. The Schleiermacher connection is itself enough to suggest that "feeling" is not to be equated simply with emotion. Thomas Silkstone has proposed that *sentiment* may be rendered more adequately as "consciousness" or "experience" (whose French equivalents Sabatier did in fact use with frequency).[45] This expanded sense of "feeling" should be kept in mind in appreciating both Sabatier and Loisy. However, while Loisy acknowledges the centrality of human experience to any adequate understanding of religion, he quickly establishes his distance from Sabatier by criticizing his overpersonalization of religion and consequent underinstitutionalization: "Religion, rather than being uniquely the religious feeling of so many individuals [and, in the case of Christianity, of being realized in the individual consciousness of Christ], is the living institution in which this feeling finds the nourishment and direction it needs" (19). The necessarily institutional nature of Christianity allows Loisy to validate the mediatorial role played by Church and dogma as preservative of the gospel message rather than deformative of it. The living character of this institution in turn validates his developmental perspective: "It is evident that a religious institution cannot remain static, because it is alive, that all movement implies change, and that all change which constitutes progress in the development of the institution ought not to be considered as a departure from its principle" (19). Here Loisy has articulated the argument that will form the core of his critique of Harnack in *L'Évangile et l'Église*. There is no pure essence of Christianity, to be recaptured from its initial form or distilled in the present from the impurities from which it has become alloyed. The gospel was inescapably Jewish in its origin, just as it had to evolve through its assimilation of Greek forms in order to remain alive. With a nod toward Newman, Loisy affirms that "life is a perpetual work of assimilation" (26).

While, against liberal Protestantism, Loisy argues that the various forms assumed by Christianity over the centuries are necessary for its continued existence, he acknowledges in principle liberal Protestantism's criticism of dogma that becomes divinized and petrified"

> In the Church, dogma would be petrified and not living if it were
> absolutely identified with its theological definition and if that were
> declared entirely immutable. Contact between criticism and
> history would be a danger to Catholics if they were obliged to
> believe that nothing had ever changed in the forms of the
> ecclesiastical constitution, beliefs or worship. (27)

Loisy's tactic is to acknowledge that the dangers of immobility and
petrification have "not always been averted on all points and in every
particular case" (28), while stressing the Church's ability to reform
itself and thereby largely escape the effects of such lapses. It is the
larger strategy, however, that is more important here. While empha-
sizing the salutary effects of dogma against Sabatier and Harnack,
Loisy uses his points of solidarity with them to suggest the inadequacies
of a *fixiste* theology in Catholicism. The preceding extract insinuates
that criticism and history are corrosive only of a certain type of apologetic. In *L'Évangile et l'Église* Loisy will argue that "the best apology for
all that lives lies in the life itself."[46] That sort of apologetic would not
be endangered by contact with critical historical methods.

Before leaving this article, it is perhaps worthwhile to raise the issue of
endangerment. Would Christianity be endangered by contact with this
form of apologetics? Without entering into the labyrinthine world of
Loisy interpretation, two summary points may be made. First, critics are
generally agreed that, for Loisy, particular developments are legitimated
by the process of development itself. But this provides little help in distinguishing true from false developments. True, Loisy borrows the language
of "preservation of the fundamental idea" and "continuity of principles"
from Newman. But neither in the more theoretical discussion in the
Firmin articles nor in the more historical treatment in *L'Évangile et l'Église*
are these criteria integrated into a historical demonstration.[47] The poten-
tial for future development becomes disconcertingly open-ended. Second,
liberal Protestantism's emphasis on religion and faith as "realities of the
moral order" (17) constitutes another point of contact—and indeed close
contact—with Loisy's own position. Despite his emphasis on "living"
dogma, he is much closer to Sabatier's symbolic reading of dogmatic
formulas, which risks volatilizing the substance of Christianity.[48]

"La définition de la religion" forms the first of three connected articles
drawn from the single chapter of the *Essais* on revelation. Its first section,
however, looks back to Sabatier and essentially retrieves themes and
develops them further. Its mode of establishing solidarity with and distance

from Sabatier is also consistent with its predecessor and could well have formed part of that article. As noted earlier, its second section picks up the theme of rationalism, alluded to at the beginning of "La théorie individualiste de la religion." Here Loisy turns to a refutation of certain rationalist objections to religion.

The universal character of religion is indicative of a kind of "religious instinct" (42) in humanity. Religion is therefore more fundamental than its expression in beliefs, more than a matter of intellect. Loisy queries:

> Is it not true that the purely rational proofs of the existence of God
> are not the sufficient principle of our faith in him; that the
> metaphysical notion of a supreme being is not the immediate
> source of our piety; that our idea of God, absolute as it may seem
> to us, is still, by its very nature, a grandiose anthropomorphism,
> and that the true God is the being whom that notion represents but
> fails entirely to express, which is to say the living God before whom
> man is conscious of his nothingness and wretchedness...? (40)

By positioning religion as not primarily intellectual but from the heart, Loisy strikes at rationalism directly, but a highly intellectualized Catholicism is implicitly in view. If a feeling for the religious is primary, then continuity resides in it rather than in the expressions of this instinct. Like the formulations of science, the symbols of religion are perfectible (35). They are susceptible to alteration and correction in their process of development, a process that includes religious ritual and institutions. Loisy makes the point by noting development from primitive to more advanced religions. But the principle would apply to development within Christianity.

The fourth and fifth Firmin articles take up core issues that will be at the heart of controversies over *L'Évangile et l'Église* and *Autour d'un petit livre.*

In "L'idée de la revelation," Loisy is concerned to hold together two elements of revealed religion while avoiding either of two extremes.[49] As a process of communication of divine truths, revelation incorporates a subjective element, insofar as the presentation of these truths must be "adapted to the general conditions of nature and human intelligence, as well as to the special and personal conditions of those who first perceived and formulated them" (60). As one who works inductively from the evidence of the biblical texts, Loisy wants to do full justice to human and historical contexts in formulating an adequate idea of revelation. At the same time he must be careful to distance himself from any charge of subjectivism, of reducing revealed truth to the level of the merely human. Here again, Auguste Sabatier is invoked as an example of what is to be avoided. Loisy fastens upon the latter part of the title in Sabatier's *Esquisse*—"Based on Psychology and History"—to position its author as putting forward no more than a history of a psychological phenomenon: "the consciousness of God in man" (45). As a process of communication of *divine* truths revelation also incorporates an objective element—while subject to immanent conditions and circumstances, revelation has a transcendent source, content, and destination (46). Here again, a cautionary note, however. Objective does not mean objectified to the point where revelation becomes identified with its expression in dogma, its intellectual dimension dominating all others.

The latter approach, then dominant in Catholic theology, has been encapsulated by Avery Dulles in his model of revelation as doctrine: "A cardinal tenet of neo-Scholasticism...is that supernatural revelation transmits conceptual knowledge by means of words (or speech)."[50] Proponents of this verbal-conceptual view of revelation tended to derive this notion from an abstract analysis of the concept of revelation in general. Revelation, then, refers to truths communicated in propositional form—either as directly formulated in scripture or in apostolic tradition, or as indirectly derived from biblical narrative or more clearly formulated by authoritative teaching, above all in church dogma. Thus, "in equating the dogmas of the church with divine revelation the neo-Scholastics are faithful to their propositional understanding of revelation. The concept of dogma as a divinely revealed truth serves in turn to reinforce the propositional view of revelation."[51]

Loisy's challenge, then, is to articulate an alternative to the equation of revelation with dogma, grounding revealed truth in life rather than in the intellect, while avoiding the charge of reductionism that he himself leveled at Sabatier. As Dulles notes, revelation for the neo-scholastic "cannot be a mere experience of feelings aroused by the innate religious sense, nor can it be given through inarticulate groans or interactions, for these signs do not convey conceptual or intellectual knowledge."[52] Loisy distinguishes among "the simple truths contained in the assertions of the faith," which are the "direct object of revelation," and the analysis and codification of these assertions in doctrine and authoritatively sanctioned dogma (48).

The "truths" invoked by Loisy function as a bridging notion, intended to connect objective to subjective, immanent to transcendent dimensions of revelation. In Wernz's estimation, for Loisy, "revelation is neither a matter of mere feeling nor a once-and-for-all deposit of dogmas. With his concept of "vérités" [truths] Loisy constructs something of an 'x' to perform the necessary mediating function between these two extremes, without much elaboration of the content of this 'x.' "[53]

In articulating his own position, Loisy's vocabulary is very unlike that of neo-scholasticism and resembles more that of Sabatier. One has the sense that Loisy is groping his way forward, having a better sense of what he wants to say than he has the precise words to say it. Loisy's preoccupation with the role of experience in revelation will lead many of his eventual critics to overlook his efforts to retain a transcendent dimension to revelation and see in his work only a Catholic form of liberal Protestantism.[54]

"Les preuves et l'economie de la révélation" ends the series of Firmin articles translated here, as it completes the more theoretical portion of Loisy's thought drawn from the *Essais d'histoire et de philosophie religieuses.* Once more Sabatier figures at the outset, providing both continuity to the series and opportunity for clarity and correction. Just as Sabatier, according to Loisy, has misunderstood the nature of religion and of revelation, so too defects in his understanding of miracle and prophecy need to be addressed. And the understanding of religion and revelation Loisy has developed in the previous two articles serves as a basis for the corrective. At issue is the current viability of the classic Catholic apologetics. He continues his strategy of remedying the defects in Sabatier's understanding by supplying a revisionist account of the questions of interest. In contrast to the prevailing Catholic conception of miracles as exterior proofs constituted by events whose extraordinary character is plain as pikestaff, and prophecies as certain witnesses to the divinely inspired character of scripture, Loisy argues that miracles and prophecies are visible only to the eyes of faith.[55] As with previous articles, emphasis has shifted from dogma and rational demonstration to experiences and life. Hence, "True religion is made to be known, tried, lived, and this personal experience has always been its true demonstration, varying in its logical expression according to the times and even to the people" (77). Consonant with the previous representations of religion and revelation, the intellectual faculty yields its primacy to a more complex notion of experience, inclusive of the intellectual dimension, yet broader and more fundamental.

In his own analysis of religious experience Dermot Lane discusses the relation between it and authority. While an emphasis on religious experience can be perceived as entailing a decreased role for ecclesiastical authority, Lane disagrees: "In fact, the more emphasis that is placed on religious experience the greater the need for some form of authority to act as a guide and interpreter of the multiple experiences that people undergo."[56] Loisy anticipates Lane's conclusion with his own assertion of the need for "an infallible Church"—but this remains more of an assertion than an argument integrated into the foregoing analysis.

In sum, while ostensibly refuting or correcting the liberal Protestantism represented by Sabatier, Loisy has introduced revisionist notions of religion, revelation, and apologetics into Catholicism. The extent of this revisionism is implied more than it is specified, the need affirmed more than the specifics of how it is to be met marked out. This same character is evident in *L'Évangile et l'Église* and accounts in significant measure for Loisy's hopes for its success and the initially favorable reception it received in some quarters.

Since Loisy's real target in his modernist writings is the theology then dominant in Catholicism, an early response to his initiatives by a representative of that theology is included here. Charles Maignen published extended critiques of both *L'Évangile et l'Église* and *Autour d'un petit livre*. Maignen's "Nouvelle théologie" is worth reading not only for its content but also for its tone. The condemnation of modernism in *Pascendi dominici gregis* cannot be really appreciated apart from the climate of fear for orthodoxy that permeated Catholicism over those years. As Maude Petre—who was in a position to know—would later write:

> We must remember, in fairness to those who were not always
> fair, that the impact of historical criticism on the traditional
> teaching of the Church was terrifying; that it seemed a case of
> saving the very essence of the Christian faith from destruction.
> Not, perhaps, since the startling revelation of Copernicanism,
> had the shock been greater.[57]

Part of Maignen's alarm stemmed from his perception that Loisy's ideas were not simply those of an isolated individual but were representative of a broader group—"of a school or, better still, a party" (99). At base, these ideas were seen to be reflective of an evolutionary naturalism, which had affinities with the errors of a number of "isms" (87). An evolutionary Catholicism was at antipodes to Maignen's representation of the traditional faith, which is essentially that of Bishop Jacques-Bénigne Bossuet. The dogmatic content is there from the beginning; only the language in which it is formulated is subject to change as the need to clarify one or another aspect of the faith emerges. The "fixism" criticized by Loisy in the Firmin articles takes articulate form in Maignen's affirmation that "in the case of the Saints and Doctors of the Church, it is certain that each of them, according to the lights he received from above, believed with an explicit and formal faith dogmas which were not defined by the Church" (91).

While there were Catholic theologians whose positions on revelation and faith, dogma and its development were more moderate than those defended by Maignen, the latter is himself no isolated figure but representative of a school that equated its theology with Catholic orthodoxy and reacted accordingly to revisionist alternatives. Maignen's contribution to this volume is to emphasize the great divide that separated the ideas of partisans of renewal from the positions they sought to revise.

The "Firmin" Articles

Alfred Loisy
Translated by Christine E. Thirlway

The Development of Christianity According to Cardinal Newman

In his work on the development of Christian doctrine (*An Essay on the Development of Christian Doctrine* [1845]), Cardinal Newman may be said to have provided a scientific theory of Catholic Christianity.[1] Newman became a Catholic while he was engaged in writing this essay, and in some ways one can trace within it the route which led him from Anglicanism to the Roman Catholic faith. Neither in that book nor in most of the works he has since published, unless perhaps in his *Grammar of Assent*, a fine treatise on religious certitude, does he confront the absolute rationalism which strikes at the very root of all positive religion. Newman is first of all an Anglican who has embraced the Catholic faith: a perfect Anglican who became a perfect Catholic when he discovered that the Catholic development was part of the true logic of Christianity, indispensable to its preservation and as divinely legitimate as Christianity itself from which it could not fundamentally be distinguished. He subjected the idea of development to a meticulous analysis, indicated those conditions which are required for normal development and which distinguish it from irregular development and from corruption, and applied it in turn to Catholicism and the Protestant sects, especially Anglicanism.

I

Newman's principal proposal is that an idea which is living, real, and nonabstract, which takes possession of men's minds, follows a line of development quite different from that taken by an axiom of geometry the conclusions of which are deduced mathematically one from another. The fortunes of such an idea depend largely on the minds that have received it and labor on it further. A relation becomes established between the idea and all the preoccupations of those who entertain it. It is as if it attracted into its orbit anything which is not contrary to it or with which it might have some positive affinity, and rejected everything not of its kind or in direct opposition. It grows by assimilating whatever surrounds it, and its purity comes not from isolating itself from everything but from dominating everything, from perpetuating itself by dominating everything which approaches it. In consequence, the history of such an idea is that of a perpetual struggle, and the times of silence are not those in which the idea flourishes and grows. Whatever risk of corruption may attend contact with the world, this risk must be run if the truth is to be understood and receive fuller manifestation. It would be quite wrong to suggest that the idea might have remained truer to itself had it more strenuously rejected all change. An idea necessarily arises from an existing state of things of which it retains the traces for a more or less extended period; it will then disengage itself from anything which may be foreign or accessory to it and, pursuing the freedom of its own expansion, gradually increase its strength; its beginnings are a measure neither of its vitality nor of its final achievement. Here below, to live is to change, and to be perfect is to have changed often. Such is the law of all real development in humanity; such is also the law of religious development.

Yet true development must be distinguished from false. The general condition for true development is *unity of type*, which must persist through all transformations which may be as considerable in their order as, in the physiological order, are those of animal life from its embryonic to its perfect state. It should be noted that one of the most common causes of corruption or false development in the religious order is the fixed determination not to follow the idea in its evolution and to enclose oneself blindly in the tradition of the past. Many heresies are born of a mistaken spirit of preservation, and such a dangerous degeneration may be less immediately visible than the change produced by true and normal development. Everything which obscures the primitive idea or is an obstacle to it, which troubles and reverses the course of development, must be not development but corruption. One cannot define as a form of corruption or decay a chronic state which acts in concert and tends to maintain the various elements of the system in equilibrium.

If the particular conditions contained in this general condition are examined in detail, it becomes apparent that the marks of true development are *preservation of the fundamental idea*, an undisputed criterion very easy to apply in the case of a philosophical doctrine, much less so in the case of a religion such as Christianity where the essential idea cannot be defined a priori because Christianity is not only an idea but an institution; *continuity of principles*, in which principles should not be confused with doctrines, for principles—for instance, the Catholic principles of hierarchy, dogma, and sacramentality—are unvarying whereas doctrines are modified in development; yet this differentiation of principles from doctrines is not absolute, and is sometimes dictated by the way we look at them, a principle being at certain times able to serve as the basis of a doctrinal development as has been the case in the Roman Church for the dogmatic principle elaborated in the doctrine of infallibility; *power of assimilation*, without which development can no more take place in the spiritual and moral order than in the physical order, the effort toward development denoting the presence of a principle which stimulates the activity of thought, and the success of the effort indicating the presence of a living idea which in a certain way reproduces itself in its acquisitions without losing its unity; *early anticipation*, meaning the fact that any particular development will at first declare itself sporadically and sketchily, not achieving its perfection until much later, because developments of an idea are in a sense no more than its various aspects asserting themselves as circumstances demand; *logical sequence*, which does not signify that the development, taken in itself and in the reality of its act, amounts merely to a syllogistic deduction, for this work is done as if spontaneously and after the event, simply through the effect of the presence of the ideas when the time comes to analyze, organize, and defend the development which has been acquired; *preservative additions*, which guarantee the preservation of the idea and of its legitimate developments, functioning in the same way as the institution of government in a growing society which would not be able to exist without its protection; finally, *chronic continuance*, true development being that which guarantees and increases the life of the idea, whereas corruption cannot but contrive and procure its ruin.

Once these principles have been established, it is easy to understand that Christianity had to have a development because it was a living fact of various aspects and a doctrine susceptible of multiple applications; because it was a universal religion which could not help but be transformed, enriched, and enlarged by its operation in relation to the world in which it was called to live; because it was impossible even for the most important items of doctrine to hold to the letter of the Scriptures without falling into a vain worship of forms; because the Scriptures propose and provoke a number of questions to which they provide no solution; because in the Scriptures themselves revelation is subject to a progressive development and there would seem to be no good reason why this development should suddenly have come to an abrupt end with the death of the last apostle; because the idea of a doctrine entirely perfect from the very beginning and having nothing to gain from subsequent investigations, applications, and experiences is inconceivable and absurd. But if the development was a necessity, so too was the authority which was to guide it, to guard it from the ever-present danger of deviation, and to provide for the preservation of what had been achieved; and this authority appeared even more indispensable to Christianity in that the latter was, and in some ways still is, responsible for its own constitution, defense, and growth. Legitimate development needs the guarantee of an infallible authority. Authority and revelation are correlative terms. Anyone who eliminates authority will be fatally thrown back on the system of natural religion, and that indeed is the end to which all the formulations of liberal Protestantism more or less openly lead. There is, therefore, a strong antecedent probability in favor of Catholic development, a probability strengthened by the fact that the development must be either accepted in its entirety or totally abandoned. It is to be expected that the historical evidence in favor of development should be uneven depending on the objects and the times: the cult of the Virgin Mary will not become widespread before that of Christ has been settled; the papacy will define itself only insofar as the Church is already consolidated. The factual evidence has itself to be illuminated by the doctrine which has emerged from it. One point of doctrine illuminates another; each testifies to all and all to each.

The particular criteria of genuine development may be recognized in the Catholic Church: the preservation of type which can be observed if one compares the Church today with the picture of the first Christians drawn by Tacitus, Suetonius, and Pliny the Younger, and with what is known about the attitude of the Church of the fourth to the sixth centuries to heresy and the barbarians; continuity of principles, among which mention must be made of the common use of the spiritual meaning of the Scriptures and the supremacy of faith over reason, which are characteristic marks of the Gospel and of Catholic Christian theology in all ages; power of assimilation, which, in combination with the preceding criterion, is to be interpreted as the conviction that opinions on religious subjects are not matters of indifference to conscience and before God, and which guarantees to the Church in the form of a legitimate development what heresy first worked out in an incomplete and irregular fashion: thus the Montanists are seen to have foreshadowed religious asceticism, the Gnostics Christian theology, Sabellius Saint Augustine's Trinitarian concept, the theology of the Church being no random combination of various opinions, but the diligent and patient elaboration of a single doctrine from very varied materials, and Catholic worship representing the sanctification by

Christianity of rites which would otherwise be without any value, and of which quite a number have been able to exist in other religions; early anticipations, of which numerous examples might be adduced, particularly in relation to Christological doctrine, from the letters of Saint Ignatius of Antioch alone; logical sequence, this relation of moral consistency which brings about the influence of one doctrine on another so that, for example, the doctrine of the divinity of Jesus Christ, given prominence by the Arian controversy, destroyed the subordinationism which had been so strongly accented in the language of the ante-Nicene Fathers, and the development of penitential discipline led to or favored infant baptism, belief in purgatory, and prayer for the dead; preservative additions, a remarkable example of which is Marian devotion, in which must be seen a development which to some extent safeguards the worship of Jesus; chronic continuance, this criterion which is at once so easy to apply to the Catholic Church and so conclusive in the light of the obstacles surmounted and the intensity of life manifested in every period right down to our own day: this to be seen against the rapid fall of philosophical systems, the immobility of the schismatic churches, the inconsistency of the Protestant confessions. The Catholic Church has been able to appropriate with impunity elements which would have been fatal to other doctrines or religious institutions: Aristotle, with the exaltation of reason, did not destroy Scholastic dogma; asceticism, which in other religions becomes the expression of a mindless fanaticism, in Catholicism holds its own as a discipline of genuine virtue and a universal service; mysticism, which elsewhere produces extravagances of doctrine and conduct, has formed great saints in the Roman Church. If Catholicism's life has sometimes seemed as if eclipsed, its wonderful revivals at the very moment when the world thought to triumph over it remain a powerful witness in favor of the system of doctrine and worship through which its development has been expressed.

II

Leaving aside this or that particular assertion whose utter exactitude might be contested from the point of view of history, the elevated philosophical value and the apologetic significance of this conception need no demonstration. Newman neither wrote nor wished to write the history of Christian development, but he has defined its idea, traced its laws, and formulated it in scientific terms; he has solved in principle all the difficulties which the theorists of individualist Christianity are at present raising against Catholic Christianity; his response is in fact principally directed at the difficulties of Anglican Protestantism. He was born into a Church possessed of a dogma, a system of worship, and a hierarchy, even though the dogma may not have been very rigorously formulated, nor the system of worship very precisely settled, nor the hierarchy solidly constituted. It seemed to him that the true spirit of traditional Christianity required that dogma should be precise, the system of worship a living one, and the ecclesiastical authority independent and sovereign within its sphere of action, and these advantages he attempted to procure for the Anglican Church by drawing on the Christian, Catholic tradition judged as distinct from the Roman tradition. His enterprise was defeated as it were simultaneously from two directions. On one flank the antitraditional and at the same time anti-Roman principle which is at the root of Anglicanism, as of all the sects issuing from the Reformation, stirred up serious opposition. He called for closer conformity with the Catholic Church, without wanting union with the papalist Church: official Anglicanism, perhaps at that time more intransigent than it now is, refused all rapprochement, and Newman was able to see that what he had dreamed of for Anglicanism was a state of affairs it would be impossible to realize: the Church was to be autonomous and independent of the civil power but not to abandon its national character; it was to have a fixed creed without an infallible authority to maintain it and resolve the issues to which it would give rise, and a truly Christian system of worship without the tradition of ecclesiastical life. On the opposite flank he was forced to acknowledge that Catholic tradition and Roman tradition had advanced at precisely the same pace, that it was impossible to separate one from the other, and that there was only one development which was Christian, legitimate, and complete, if not absolutely perfect and definitive in all its parts, the Roman Catholic development. Anglicanism could no longer make up even some portion of the true Church of Jesus Christ, which was one and indistinguishable from the Roman Church. In his book on the development of Christianity, Newman put down the results of his trials and sealed them with his conversion.

As his criticism of Anglicanism strikes not merely at the defects of the Established Church but also at the very principle of Protestantism, and his analysis of Christian development was conceived in opposition to this principle, he answers the objections of the most radical Protestantism. He saw, just as clearly as the Protestant scholars who have written recently on the subject of the history of Christian dogmas and the philosophy of religion, that when the Savior was put to death, the apostles had neither a clearly defined organization nor a fixed creed, nor a program of religious action or worship to institute. From the Gospel they had heard and from their fidelity to it, from the loose association which they had formed at the beginning and to which Jesus' choosing had given a rudiment of constitution, from the baptismal rite and from the unforgettable memory of the Last Supper, under the influence of the events which followed the Passion, that is, the appearances of the risen Christ and the consolidation of the faith among the disciples, the first persecutions, Paul's conversion and the preaching of the Gospel to the Gentiles, issued the Apostolic Church, from which came forth, in due course, under the influence of other demands and other circumstances, the Catholic Church with its hierarchy ever more distinct, its dogma ever more defined and developed, its ritual ever more ceremonial and complicated. However, although Newman perceived the whole range of this development, he did not lay enormous stress on its first beginnings. It was the principle of development itself which he wanted to see accepted and, for him, the precise determination of what properly belonged to the primitive foundations of Christianity, or to the earliest layers of Christian development, was secondary: difficult as they may be to establish with certainty, these historical details are unimportant from the religious point of view; everything which the critic may discover in this order of research is already accounted for in the theory of development. In the same way, because Anglicanism is quite willing to acknowledge the principle of a social organization of Christianity, Newman did not emphasize the necessity of conceiving Christianity as a religious society but laid the greatest stress on the necessity for hierarchical development in such a society.

In order to allow the theory of development its proper amplitude by extending the historical base without which it would be nothing, its principle needs to be more explicitly drawn out and applied, in greater detail than was done by Newman himself, to the whole of the history of religion since the origins of humanity. This principle, which he applied mainly to the history of Christianity in relation to the Gospel, also applies to the Gospel in relation to Judaism and to the Mosaic religion in relation to what preceded it. For Christianity is in a very true sense a development from postexilic Judaism, which is a development from the religion of the prophets, which is a development from primitive Mosaic Yahwism, which is a development from the religion of the patriarchs, which had its beginnings in the religion of prehistoric humanity. The great moments of revelation which mark the different phases of this development do not upset its continuity; on the contrary, they guarantee it, because these are not revolutions which destroy the work of the past in order to introduce a new religion, but due and proper transformations in which the religious tradition takes advantage of the light of a new day, increases its vitality, broadens its action. On the manner in which revelation itself enters into the development and fastens itself to it, Newman is less than explicit. This is certainly not because he was afraid to come to grips with the problem; it was rather that the question did not present itself to him in the terms in which it now presents itself to contemporary theology following the critical effort of the last fifty years. The biblical question seems to have been among the least of his preoccupations, unless at the end of his life, and it is in relation to the Bible that the problem of divine revelation demands the attention of the philosopher and the historian. What he wrote on the inspiration of the Scriptures shows that his thought was sensitive to the subject but shows also that he had not found a satisfactory formula—if that was what he was looking for—to express the relation between divine revelation and biblical inspiration, and the relation of both to the religious development which was accomplished before the birth of the Church.

Even insofar as concerns Christian development, he might be reproached for having seemed so often to reduce it to the movement of ideas, the progress of belief, the definition of dogmas. The very title of his book seems to indicate that in his mind it is above all the idea of doctrine which is to be associated with that of development. Yet this is hardly more than a superficial impression the reason for which is easy to guess. In every completed development one has to distinguish a threefold moment: first of all the actual fact or act of development, the living and, one might almost say unconscious phenomenon of a belief which becomes stronger and spreads, of moral principles which acquire a wider and more fertile application, of an authority which increases its influence and transforms its mode of action, of a system of worship which undertakes new practices— all this may be called the *real* moment of development; then, through the partial resistance which makes it the subject of argument and provokes its justification, the development becomes the focus of deeper reflection: this is the *theological* moment of the development, which in important matters leads to the *dogmatic* moment, that is, the formal consecration of the development by a decision of the Church. This definition regularizes the development and specifies its formulation on the particular point treated by the definition, a point which will either remain simply acquired, because the vital movement bears away on another course, or serve as the basis for a new development. Because every particular development finds its expression in the teaching of the Church and places itself in the framework of the official theology, one is tempted to present the whole of Christian development as a movement of ideas culminating in definitions and doctrinal classification. Yet at base there is something other and much greater than a movement of ideas; there is the entire life of the Church. This Newman saw and expressed better than anyone before him.

III

It is worth mentioning, and demonstrates the total honesty of this great spirit, that Newman did not claim to have drawn his theory of Christian development from tradition, even though he could well have found some trace of it, some "early anticipation," in the literature of the Church; the only authors he cites as having put forward the same idea before him are Joseph de Maistre and Möhler; he observes that theologians adopt it implicitly and without suspecting what they are doing; he does not in fact present his theory as a properly theological concept: he calls it a hypothesis to account for a difficulty, but it would be just as unreasonable to reject this hypothesis in theology as to contest those of Galileo and Newton in astronomy; novelty is no more acceptable an objection to the law of development than it succeeded in being to that of gravitation; in one case as in the other, the hypothesis, instead of having been deduced from previously accepted doctrines, is put forward to explain the facts to which those doctrines relate or to explain the very production of the doctrines. Newman fully understood the logical significance of his theory and how it differed from that of Vincent de Lérins, if this be reduced to the abstract idea of an entirely doctrinal development, of a simple labor of dialectic on preexistent material, of a perfecting of the formulas by means of logical distinctions and a special terminology. It would not have occurred to him that it might be considered daring on his part thus to offer traditional theology unsolicited assistance. He simply considered that "Catholicism ran the risk of having a new world to conquer, without yet possessing the weapons indispensable for warfare, while unbelief already had its views and its conjectures on which it arranged the facts of ecclesiastical history and even found supporting proof of its negative conclusions in the absence of any scientific theory among the defenders of the tradition."* Half a century has passed since Newman, still a neophyte

---

* See John Henry Newman, *Essay*, 28–29 (ed. 1845).

in the Catholic Church, gave rein to his devotion in expressing this
apprehension; the new world of which he spoke has become yet larger
and has been explored still further; the scientific knowledge of the origins
of Christianity, and indeed of the origins and history of all the religions,
has made enormous progress; the conquest dreamed of by his apostolic
soul has not yet been accomplished, for it is a conquest which needs to
be constantly pursued, but it may be said that thanks to him it is carried
on under more advantageous conditions.

Can theology use without fear the instrument he bestowed on it and
himself used so admirably? It has been said recently that "people like
Möhler and Newman, unable to avoid admitting that Catholicism today
is no longer what it was in the first centuries, have made this strange
concession to history, applying the theory of evolution to dogmas."* If
the writer had read Newman, he would have discovered that Newman
never sought to avoid admitting any truth whatsoever, and that he had
made the discovery in question before he became a Catholic. His purpose
was not to make a concession but simply to explain history by outlining
his theory of Christian development, and he did not dream of sacrificing
the least iota of Catholic tradition. He would have thought "strange" the
astonishment professed by the Protestant critic and would have added
the final straw by demonstrating to him, in the *Essay on the Development*,
that the theory applied not only to dogmas but to the entire Catholic
institution. In spite of which, Newman did not think his system in any
way open to criticism from an orthodox point of view, nor that any part
of it contradicted either the positive facts of tradition or the common
teaching of theologians.

He himself would undoubtedly agree that his theory is not a traditional doctrine, but a hypothesis of the scientific order, and many Catholics
might be tempted to ask him since when hypotheses of this type have
been entitled to prevail over one or other manner of looking at the facts
recommended at least implicitly by tradition. To be freely welcomed in
theology, should not a doctrine comply with the axiom *quod semper, quod
ubique, quod ab omnibus* [what (has been held) always, everywhere, by every-
body]? To this objection Newman would certainly have replied that his
case was not new in the history of theology but one that had occurred on
several occasions since the beginning, since a true religion had existed,
and since there had been a Christian theology. The idea of development

---

* A. Sabatier, *Esquisse d'une philosophie de la religion*, 299.

as he understood it has not yet taken possession of theology, that is, it is not reckoned among the official theses of Catholic teaching; it is, nonetheless, in a very real fashion dominant in the tradition, since everything has always taken place as if it had been believed, since the Church has never ceased to develop, without hesitation or scruple, in the manner described by Newman and since the entire history of the Church is here as witness to the theory. It has therefore been adopted implicitly and equivalently without as yet experiencing the need of explicit formulation; now that the need exists, the formulation has come to birth; it is still as yet perfectible, and that will follow; but it should not be condemned as absolutely new; it is no more than the expression, appropriate to the state of modern knowledge, of tradition itself and of Christianity, as their history, their documents, show them to be. If it has not yet found a place in the manuals of theology, everything suggests that it soon will, and that its place there will be no less secure than that of other notions, also scientific in origin, which have determined the orientation of theology at decisive moments of Christian development. Is it not evident, in a sense, that the idea of the Logos, before its entry into the fourth Gospel, into the apologetics of the Fathers and into Christian theology of the third century was also a scientific theory? Is it not true that the idea of consubstantiality, before being canonized at Nicea, and the idea of transubstantiation, before being applied to the Eucharist, were purely scientific notions? Was not the idea of the native corruption of human nature which Saint Augustine elaborated in his theory of grace rooted as much in a philosophical doctrine as in the Scriptures? Is not the theory of human society and its constitutive elements a matter for science, and has it not nonetheless been felicitously drawn upon by the modern theologians to establish the notion of the Church? In their day, all these scientific theories may be said to have strengthened and even, historically speaking, saved traditional Christianity: so will it be said of the theory of development that it intervened at the proper time to illuminate religion's past and prepare its future, by explaining how there could and was bound to emerge from the Gospel, without corruption of its identity, but by a sort of progressive affirmation of that identity in a sustained flowering, Catholic Christianity with all the phases of its transformations and of its growth, with all the acquisitions which have enlarged its life and in the end achieved expression as dogma.

In appropriating and transforming for its own use the scientific notions that seemed best to express its thought and its life, the Church has discarded more than one inadequately formulated fragment of incomplete doctrine which tradition had previously carried without repugnance and sometimes even with a certain approval. A case in point is the *subordinationism* of the ante-Nicene Fathers which was mentioned earlier as having disappeared with the definition of *consubstantial*. Newman had many other examples at his disposition and knew full well that development produces a kind of wastage, the discarding of everything which in ideas, language, and customs might form an obstacle to the burgeoning life which constitutes this development itself. He therefore foresaw that his theory, when it should be incorporated into Catholic teaching, would not fail to do away with some less than perfect views, and that the first of these would be a confused and abstract manner of looking at the history of religion, a manner which has become closely associated with the fundamental ideas of authority, unity, and perpetuity, essential attributes of the Christian tradition, but which may also be perfected without the slightest damage to these principles, and which indeed must be so perfected in order that the principles may be preserved. In Newman's thought, for a theory to be orthodox, it is enough that it should not contradict any dogma but, on the contrary, adapt itself to all, and that orthodoxy should have need of it in order to become fully aware of its own history and state. The theory of development provides, and is alone in providing, a satisfactory explanation of the changes which have occurred in Catholic Christianity since the beginning and which occur daily under our very eyes and demand that rational and scientific explanation; otherwise all these changes would turn into invincible objections against a Church whose glory is to have preserved intact the deposit of the Gospel, uncorrupted and always keeping the same identity. What the theory opposes can only be an antihistoric conception of the perpetual identity of Christianity, according to which the development of the hierarchy would consist only in acknowledging by solemn canons a factual situation and rights which had always been in existence in the particular form those canons establish; the development of dogma in finding clearer terms and more explicit formulations than the words and formulations of old; the development of the system of worship in giving official sanction to practices current from the beginning or in allowing them a wider range. It is clear that according to the theory and, Newman would not have hesitated to add, according to history, the development of Christianity cannot be reduced merely to a process of perfecting ecclesiastical language, a work of logical deduction or a multiplication of like practices, but that the development must be conceived as intimate, vital, real, as considerable in its order as that of animal life from birth to the adult state, implying, in consequence, the identity of the subject through all the transformations which take place in it according to the law of its institution, but excluding as a state of death, absolute immutability in the form once acquired. When it is said that the sign of the Catholic Church's divinity is that it always keeps the same identity in its organization, its doctrine, and its action, this should be understood as the living unity, the real continuity, the perfect equilibrium of its development through the ages. Should one understand that identity in a totally coarse and material sense, as if it were that of a statue which had continued to exist for hundreds of years without deteriorating, one would certainly fail to make contact with the Church's thought and would be committing an error pregnant with innumerable others. Up to the present the Catholic Church has not reflected a great deal on her history, having always had better things to do; she has defined nothing, she gives no positive teaching on the mode of her development; she simply maintains, following the witness the Holy Spirit affords her, that everything out of which she lives, which is to say her hierarchical institution, her dogma, and her system of worship, is consonant with the Gospel, and in all this she is aware of herself as the living prolongation of the Gospel; when she maintains the identity of the Gospel today with that of yesterday, the Catholic Church of the nineteenth century with the Church of the Apostles, it is not at all her purpose to speak of an identity entirely material and external, but of a substantial identity, one might say a personal identity, perfectly compatible in the Church, as in all living creatures, with a genuine development of the organism and an increasing manifestation of power and activity. The preservation of dogmas *in eodem sensu eademque sententia* [in the same meaning and in the same purport] excludes from doctrinal development contradiction, the substitution of one meaning for another under the same form of words but not the interpretation of a traditional truth by means of notions connatural, if one may be allowed so to express it, to the first expression of those truths. Since the end of the first century, what has Christian theology been if not a constant and ever-renewed effort to establish a sort of equation or perpetual correspondence between the interpretation of the revealed dogmas and the intellectual progress of humanity?

Such is Cardinal Newman's theory on Christian development, insofar as we have understood it. We shall not permit ourselves to appraise it from a theological point of view, or rather we should deem it rash to appraise it otherwise than its author has thought fit to do. It seemed useful, by means of a brief analysis, to bring it to the attention of the readers of this *Revue* so as to show that a broad conception of the history of dogmas and of Christian development, a conception truly scientific in which all the legitimate conclusions of historical criticism may find a refuge, was formulated by a Catholic thinker well in advance of certain Protestant publications which have made a stir in recent times. Mr. Harnack's *History of Dogmas*[2] is more erudite than the *Essay on the Development of Christian Doctrine*; but how much inferior in its general understanding of Christianity and of the multiplicity of its life, of the intimate relation which exists between each of the forms and phases of that life! As for those who have read the *Outlines of a Philosophy of Religion*, by Mr. A. Sabatier, and who may have been struck by certain insights and perhaps regretted that no analogous book should have been written in defense of Catholicism, they can now be told that such a book does exist, better documented than that of the learned dean of the Faculty of Protestant Theology and founded on a more complete religious experience, by a more open and more impartial spirit. In our times, Catholic theology has been granted the great Doctor of whom it was in need. In this Doctor neither devotion to the Church nor a feeling for traditional orthodoxy was missing (it is hardly thinkable that anyone would be so mischievous as to quibble over his mistaken opinion on the *obiter dicta* of the Scriptures); nor any particle of the scientific spirit, nor ardor and fertility in labor, nor indeed afflictions. Perhaps what was missing was a few disciples.

The Individualist Theory of Religion

Whether it be represented by Voltaire or Renan, French rationalism finally comes down to the cult of pure reason or the religion of science. Rather different from this superficial rationalism is the religious concept, largely Germanic in origin and character, which we find professed by a large number of Protestant scholars who, having broken with the dogmatic tradition, claim to retain religion if not as a visible, social institution then at least as a real and necessary part of man's spiritual activity, a part which is distinct from philosophy and from science and which has been displayed in its highest form on earth, its unique and salvific model, in a word its revelation, in the Christ.

I

These scholars—let us simply mention Mr. A. Harnack in Germany and in France Mr. A. Sabatier—criticize all beliefs not excepting the beliefs of Christianity; they do not accept miracles in the ordinary theological sense; on issues of biblical literature and history they are more or less in agreement with unbelieving rationalists; but they affirm God, religion, and faith as realities of the moral order. It is hard to be certain precisely what they mean by these three moral entities. Their creed appears to consist of a single article whose significance is not otherwise defined: man is saved, which is to say morally regenerated, by faith in God the Father revealed to him in Jesus. This formula for religion and Christianity would seem to be the final, legitimate, and logically inevitable expression of the true principle of the Reformation which excludes all external authority, the Church, tradition, the letter of the Scriptures, and recognizes no rule of faith other than the interior light of the spirit discerning God's word in the Scriptures. The Bible is not an authority for faith: this comes to birth spontaneously in the soul through contact with the divine word contained in the Bible. For the Bible, as a book, is not in itself that word but only inasmuch as it awakens, in human souls, faith in God the Father revealed by Jesus. The authority of the Scriptures is therefore less than relative; it consists simply in the fact that the Sacred Books are the ordinary source of the purest religious impressions and the most complete religious experience. This is proposed as the essential doctrine of the Reformation and also as pure Christianity. In this fashion it is intended that religion should escape the control of tradition and science, the tyranny of authority, and the indiscreet curiosity of criticism.

It is certainly true that this pure Christianity is pure Protestantism. The idea of it seems at first to be quite positive, but it has negative implications. Mr. Harnack and Mr. Sabatier are right to consider themselves heirs to the true spirit of Luther; like him they teach salvation by faith alone, even though on the subject of God, Jesus, faith, and salvation, Luther held doctrines less distant than theirs from traditional teaching; and they agree once again with him in their exclusion of all that is not purely evangelical, all that was not formally taught, organized, or instituted by Jesus, although Luther thought the Gospel contained a great many things which these modern disciples claim not to see in it. If to be Protestant is to lay down the rules of one's religion oneself with the help of the Gospel, and not to be Catholic, then these theologians are the most perfect Protestants ever seen.

But is it not an abuse of language, a philosophical error, and a complete misunderstanding of history to present in the name of religion and Christianity something which is in itself, leaving aside the essential negation attached to the positive part of the doctrine, no more than a partial, incomplete, and insufficient definition of the Christian religious consciousness? Religion has never been conceived as something entirely personal to the individual, a mere psychological operation of which each person is both subject and judge. The direct and constant relationship religion establishes between man and God has always been regarded as implying at the same time an effective bond between man and his own kind. To say religion is to say the opposite of individualism. Religion, in all its forms, even the most imperfect, has always sought the union of men in God, not merely the union of man with God. And what may be said of all religion must also be said of Christianity above all. This is why, in history, everything that has borne the name of religion has been, in one way or another, an institution. This is why Christianity as well, when it ceased to be the hope of Israel, when by the death and the resurrection of the Savior it became a religion distinct from the Jewish religion, was also an institution. This is why the Reformers of the sixteenth century, while proposing the principle of individualism so as to be able to evade the Church's authority, felt obliged, in order to preserve something of the religion and the Christianity they did not want to abandon, to make Protestantism itself an institution and to provide their individual Christianity with a social form. This is why the new Doctors feel bound to recognize that it is "in organized religious societies, in their institutions, common worship, liturgy and rules of faith and of discipline that religion brings its fundamental principle to objective realisation, shows forth the soul within it and develops all its power."*

Now if religion, rather than being uniquely the religious consciousness of so many individuals, is the living institution in which this consciousness finds the nourishment and direction it needs, Christianity, which undoubtedly is and intends to be a religion, must of necessity be a religious institution; if it is bound to be a religious institution, it can be neither summed up in a sentiment nor defined in a single formula; even though it draws all its energies from its originator, and was to all intents and purposes realized in Jesus, it could not be wholly realized, factually and historically, in an individual conscience, even though this conscience should be that of Christ, nor confine itself to the communication of the sentiment which came to birth in that conscience. Apart from the fact that such communication cannot be conceived without reference to the exterior means which procures it and which, being indispensable, must form part of the true notion of religion, it is evident that a religious institution cannot remain static, because it is alive, that all movement implies change, and that no change which constitutes progress in the development of the institution should be considered as a departure from its principle; as long as the Christian institution continues to perform the work of the Gospel, as long as it transforms itself solely in the interests of performing this task better, it will remain within the spirit and intentions of Jesus, it will be true Christianity, and to undertake its destruction in the cause of a better restoration of the Gospel will be to pursue a dangerous illusion, since the Gospel could exist only once in its native form, and this form, with the best will in the world, cannot be restored.

II

In the system we are discussing, religion, rightly construed, is supposed to have begun only with Jesus and one might almost say also finished with

---

* Sabatier, *Esquisse d'une philosophie de la religion*, 405.

him. It is of course asserted that man has always been religious, but man and religion are regarded as products of the evolution which is the law of the universe; religion arises in man from his sense of powerlessness faced by "universal determinism," a sense which he overcomes by "a return to the very principle on which our being depends and by a moral act of faith in the origin and the purpose of life"; the sense of this powerlessness and the liberating effort of faith have become refined with the passing of time; in the beginning man peopled the universe with spirits which he imagined were attached, like souls to bodies, sometimes to a weird object, sometimes to a natural phenomenon: this is animism; he then separated the spirit from its usual habitation: this was the beginning of polytheism and idolatry; introducing among the gods the hierarchy which had been established in human societies, he moved toward monotheism and, insofar as he himself became a moral being, made his gods moral; however, this tendency toward moral monotheism did not reach its climax in the Indo-European family because in the mythology of that race it came up against an insurmountable obstacle; it achieved its end only in Israel, "thanks to the particular spiritual bent of the Hebrew family" whose "primitive polytheism was of an abstract character," and thanks most of all to the prophets, originators of an "essentially individualist reformation" which made of a particular god "the God of moral conscience, invisible creator of all things, judge and rewarder of all human consciences"; this God still remained "exterior to the conscience, the image of holiness awakened in souls the consciousness of sin, and gave rise to a tragic conflict between the human will, enslaved to evil, and the divine law, intransigent by its very character"; in Jesus, "God would become interior to the conscience and reveal himself in man's own self, as the principle of justification and salvation"; thus "the Heavenly Father becomes incarnate in the Son of Man," and thereby comes to pass "that religious consummation of the divine and the human seeking and calling to each other in the obscure desire of the conscience"; unfortunately, dogma and the Church, thrusting themselves between the conscience and God, reestablished the barrier that Jesus had overthrown; through them "salvation is compromised" and "perfect religion disappears."*

Much more evident than Mr. Sabatier's conclusion is the fact that the Savior himself did not conceive of the relationship between God and the human conscience as it is presented in the new theory. However

---

* Sabatier, *Esquisse*, 22, 123–25, 155, 191.

sensitive the Heavenly Father may be to the heart of Jesus, the essential distinction of God from man, of the divine from the human, is clearly affirmed in the Gospel, and it is not the historical Jesus who is said to have claimed that the Heavenly Father had become incarnate in him. Such an expression is just as unacceptable to an accurate criticism as to traditional orthodoxy. The religion of the Gospel is certainly not that psychological pantheism, that subjective worship, that apotheosis of the conscience. In the Gospel God is interior to the soul and dwells there; but he nonetheless remains the God who causes the sun to shine and the rain to fall, whose kingdom comes, who must be looked for if we are to avoid being caught unawares by his judgment. He is immanent to the soul and transcendent to the world. By what right do we take only one half of the sentiment which prevails in Christ's preaching and falsify this half by neglecting the other? Is the "tragic conflict" of the sinful will and the divine law in the religion of the prophets really so sharply defined, and did Jesus have to feel it in order to bring it to an end? Is one to make him a sinner so as to be more certain of his being a Lutheran? Were the prophets and Jesus really the fathers of religious individualism? There is a sense in which the prophets rely on their inspiration alone and Jesus on the intimate revelation of God within his soul; but would it not be better still to say that the prophets and Jesus rely on God who sends them, for they are not *subjectivists*; and what is it they want if not to restore, strengthen, and perfect the tradition? The prophets do not consciously preach a religion different from the one imposed on their forefathers, and Jesus claims to have come not to destroy the Law and the Prophets but to fulfill them. Is it necessary to add that they believed they were advancing the development of God's kingdom, not performing certain psychological experiments from which posterity might profit? The specific purpose of the prophets was to procure the faithfulness of a people to its God; that of Jesus was to create faith in the kingdom which had been foretold by the prophets and which he himself had brought on to earth. It is a wanton violation of their thought and an arbitrary interpretation of their intentions, to detach them from the past with which they are in continuity and from the works they perform, to make of them the precursors of a religious theory invented in our own day. They lived the religion traditional to their nation, they lived it, and Jesus may be said to have transfigured it in living it: but the religion which lived in them was not merely an individual sentiment, it was the living religion of Israel and of the world, institution and faith, reality and hope, a religious life both complete and progressive, all for each and each for everyone, in which each person shares in the universal communion. Religion, the heavenly kingdom, God, are for them realities at once intimate and external, subjective and objective, which they carry in themselves and within which they move. They do not serve a sentiment or an abstraction but the living God and the work he wishes to accomplish through them, that is, the coming of his kingdom, the constitution of the society of the just. Teaching us to feel conscious of God is only a small part of their program: this is the very most one can say, seeing that they do not speak of feeling but of knowing, loving, and serving the Creator.

And in that dim past which one divides in so Scholastic a fashion into superimposed compartments: fetishist animism, polytheism, monolatry, and monotheism, might not something more be seen than the as yet imperfect and so imperfectly known workings of religious thought? Whatever may have been said of it, semitic polytheism was not in the least abstract, but included families and hierarchies of gods; the vague notion of holiness had been attributed to other gods besides the God of Israel; the very special predispositions of the Hebrew people to monotheism largely escape the historian, and Mr. Sabatier would have done better not to borrow Renan's curious theory of patriarchal elohism; Israelite monotheism had to overcome mythology and idolatry; if modern science fails to provide the natural explanation of that success, its incapacity still should not allow a misreading of the historical circumstances involved. But without for the moment insisting on all these points, let us recall a universal fact whose significance can escape neither the historian nor the philosopher: just as religion, in all its forms and in every age and every country, has always been social, so has it always been *objective*; it has placed God close to man but above him; it is founded on a real distinction between God and man. Humanity's continuing effort to reach God is invincible evidence that God exists: yet this would represent no more than centuries of misconstruction and illusion if, in order to reach God, man had only to gaze at himself and reflect that the entire reality of God consisted in the idea he made of him, all religion in the feelings he cherished for this ideal. It is precisely because religion has an objective reality that dogma and the Church are not, for the Catholic, annoying intermediaries which deprive him of God and religion; for him they are not things alien to religion, since they are religion, since they reveal God; and yet the dogma and the Church are not things alien to the believer himself either, dogma because he lives from it, the Church because he is part of it.

III

The Church may be even more readily excused for not having managed to preach pure religion, in that the Gospel itself, according to the learned advocates of individualist Christianity, does not contain it unmixed. In the same way as Christianity, they tell us, received Greek and pagan forms in the Church, in the Gospel it had a specifically Jewish form: for the Savior did not find it sufficient simply to feel within himself the "consummation of the religious union of the divine and the human," he believed himself to be, he said he was, the Messiah, and this is a Jewish concept, not a religious idea of universal validity; he proclaimed the final judgment, the resurrection of the dead, all Jewish beliefs which our learned critics consider immaterial to religion and faith; he spoke of the Pentateuch as a historical book written by Moses, and the Psalms as the work of David; in brief, on many occasions he showed himself Jewish in spirit and in practice, even though he is supposed not to have been so at heart; if therefore one wants to arrive at pure Christianity, one must divest it of its first wrapping, which is Jewish, as Jesus was by the fact of his birth and education; just as, if the Church of Rome were the only Christian confession and the Gospels had disappeared, and if true Christianity had not have been discovered half by Luther, and wholly by the modern heirs to his thought, one would still be able to retrieve it by divesting it of its Catholic wrapping.

That, however, would be a delicate operation, and, without wishing to offend the eminent men who engage in it in good faith, one may be permitted to think them incapable of succeeding. For what is involved is not really an individual task or particular work which has to be done once and for all thereafter never to require attention again. Let us not discuss the appreciation of the Jewish elements claimed to be present in the Savior's preaching, or of what may be taken to be purely Israelite in his mode of existence during his ministry; let us say rather, without going into these details, that the whole Gospel is Jewish in the sense that it was conditioned by Judaism and adapted to the circles in which it was preached. It could have been no other on pain of failing to be alive, nor could it stay as it was on pain of dying in the very place where it had been born. But for its life to continue, was it necessary for ingenious philosophers to examine the Gospels for what was purely universal and what purely Jewish, reject the latter and retain the former, and draw up for the apostles a short creed to include only the essence of what seems to our critics to be the perfect religion? It hardly needs saying that on this hypothesis, Christianity would have expired even more surely and promptly than if it had kept the whole of its Jewish form, and that it would have disconcerted its preachers before disheartening its hearers. The living Gospel was neither usefully able nor in duty bound to transform itself in the external forms it took, in the way it treated the Gentiles and organized and interpreted itself, other than in accordance with the new circumstances imposed upon it by events and by its own expansion; it adapted itself to those circumstances bit by bit as they arose, not through human, political reflection, but through a kind of intimate necessity, more or less felt, which made it develop whatever, in its current state of being, favored its progress, and correct anything through which it would have been hindered or compromised. The life of a religion never consists in seeking to discover a quintessence, but in its action on souls; and everything which advances this action, everything which religion draws into its orbit and uses for its own ends, participates in its life insofar as it serves that end. The question therefore is not to discover how to define the essence of Christianity or of the Gospel, for no absolute definition is possible, since Christianity is a living reality and not a concept of the mind; it is communicated by being described such as it is; if one insists on giving it a scientific form, one creates an abstract symbol which has in itself no religious effect, because such is not the property of abstractions. The question is to discover where the living Gospel is, where it has been ever since it began, where it continues to be today. It is a question of fact, not one of logical subtleties. In any case, one should not talk about a return to pure Christianity in the sense in which pure is used by our learned critics because, on their own admission, such a Christianity has never existed. Is one then to create it today by scientific means, and if one were to do so would this intellectual product be a living religion? This we are entitled to doubt, given that no religion ever has been founded in this manner.

It does not surprise us to learn that Christianity did not remain *pure* after Jesus: it kept to the laws of its institution. Nor are we much scandalized to hear that Christianity became pagan in Catholicism, as it had been Jewish in the Gospel; that ecclesiastical dogma is "a material Greek, in form, in color and in every fiber of its tissue"; that the constitution of the Church is the "perfect mirror of the very constitution of the Roman Empire, the parish being modeled on the *municipe* (!)and the diocese on the province (!), the archdiocese on the great prefectures and, rising at the top of the pyramid, the bishop of Rome and the papacy whose ideal dream is none other than, in the religious order, the universal and absolute monarchy of which the Caesars had provided the first image"; that monastic asceticism together with the celibacy of the clergy and the exaltation of virginity are "the consequences (?) of a dualism and of the imitation of an ideal which, having come from the Orient, seduced the feverish imaginations of an expiring world"; that in the Church's worship could be seen "to reappear the ancient hierarchy of gods, demigods, heroes, nymphs or goddesses, replaced by the Virgin Mary, angels, demons (!) and saints," together with "all the superstitions including the most naive fetishism, pilgrimages, rosaries and litanies, veneration of images and relics, signs of the cross, rites and sacraments conceived and celebrated after the manner of the ancient mysteries."*

Mr. Sabatier, who ventures these historical opinions, neither particularly nor entirely new and altogether too hasty, sees dogma in the light of its philosophic content while failing to take account of its spirit; he seems to be less than vaguely familiar with the origin of ecclesiastical boundaries, the development of Christian asceticism, and the effective role of the bishop of Rome during the first centuries of the Church; he chooses to see only the external forms of worship, without bothering himself over the meaning the Church attaches to them. But let us for the time being leave on one side these errors which often amount to injustice, in order to concentrate on the general and incontestable fact of the actual adaptation of Christianity to Greek science, to the conditions of the Roman State, to the religious spirit of the nations converted or to be converted. Nothing was more legitimate in itself nor more essential to the progress of the religion. Does not Mr. Harnack himself† recognize that the theological work of the first centuries, in which Origen was the principal workman, was in its time indispensable to the conversion of the Greco-Roman world, that the Nicean definition saved Christianity, and that the triumph of Arius would have been its ruin, just as he recognizes that the future of Catholicism was essentially tied to the definition of pontifical infallibility by the Vatican Council. The elements of ancient philosophy appropriated by Christianity in order to interpret its faith, the governmental organization it assumed in developing the rudiment of constitution it had preserved from its origins, the external forms of its worship which had become more complicated and more solemn than they had been at the beginning, the homage paid to the Virgin and to the saints, are all these to be condemned simply on the grounds that they did not exist (and how could they have existed?)

---

* Sabatier, *Op. Cit.*, 232–34.

† Harnack, *Lehrbuch der Dogmengeschichte*, 3rd ed., vol. 1: 590, 603; vol. 2: 217; vol. 3: 768.

in the Galilean Gospel? If the whole of this development is animated by the spirit of the Gospel, if it is necessary to its preservation and its dissemination, if it serves to promote the religion of Jesus, what more is there to say? If we reproach the Catholic Church for all these things, do we not reproach it for having lived at all and for continuing to live now? And if the Church had not lived, where would the Gospel be now? Our learned critics, intrepid logicians, misinterpret the most basic law of the created world, that is, that life is a perpetual work of assimilation. This error corresponds remarkably well to the one they commit in persuading themselves that, in order to strengthen Christianity one simply has to pare it down.

IV

We are assured that the religious revolution inaugurated by Luther, the scientific revolution inaugurated by Copernicus and Galileo, the revolution in criticism brought about by the introduction of the historical method and its numerous discoveries have ruined the authority of the Church, the authority of dogma, and the authority of the Scriptures to such a degree that Catholic Christianity, founded on that triple authority, must now be without means of support, poised on the edge of the abyss. Having thought to disclose not only Catholicism's difference from the Gospel, but also its essential opposition to it, and to demonstrate the paganization of Christianity in the Church by the confusion of hierarchical authority over the conscience with the authority of God, the confusion of faith with intellectual knowledge in the religious order, the confusion of God's mysterious action in souls with the magic of ancient cults, these learned men have no hesitation in holding the Pope to be the Antichrist, and the Roman Church the Beast of the Apocalypse. According to them, the criticism provides sufficient justification for the Protestant thesis in its newest form: "salvation* by faith regardless of beliefs," and for the rebuttal of what they claim as the Catholic thesis: salvation by absolute submission to the authority of the Church. They concede that well-disposed souls may still find religion in the Church, because the latter has not deprived them of the Gospel. But it is not the Church herself who gains this advantage for them: the Roman Church is a political

---

* Sabatier, *Op. Cit.*, 406n.

institution founded on religion which it uses to make its living, an institution which maintains its credit in ways all too human, among which ignorance, superstition, and diplomatic cunning predominate. As for the poor Catholics, they have to be convinced of their incompetence in religious matters and to refrain from examining in detail the dogmas which they accept en bloc. If once they tried to take proper account of them they would no longer be able to believe what they are taught. "Thus the dogma is saved," writes Mr. Sabatier, "but at what a price. They make it divine and then petrify it."*

This scornful evaluation is not without its logic. It has only one fault: it fails to correspond to the actual facts. In the Church, dogma would be petrified and not living if it were absolutely identified with its theological definition and if that were declared entirely immutable. Contact between criticism and history would be a danger to Catholics if they were obliged to believe that nothing had ever changed in the forms of the ecclesiastical constitution, beliefs, or worship. If everything in the Church were to be subordinated to the temporal interest of its hierarchy or even to the prestige of its authority, the Church would not be a Christian institution. But the Church neither teaches nor holds that its dogmatic definitions are the sufficient and absolutely perfect expression of the supernatural realities they represent; she establishes them as the best and only ones suitable to the time at which she defines and uses them; she does not consider them immutable or beyond improvement in every aspect, for she has constantly been engaged and is still engaged daily in their completion, explanation, and ever more precise definition and clarification and in improving them by means of all these additions, explanations, and definitions: the perpetual work of theology and dogmatics which goes on in the Church is no more than a continuing effort toward a closer and closer and better and better adaptation of the doctrinal expression of the divine truth, which alone is in itself perfect and alone unchanging, to the current and varying needs of humanity; dogmatic definitions cut away precisely those errors in view of which they are promulgated, they do not express all aspects and all consequences of the truths they attest; thus the field remains open to progress, to work, to the life of the intellect in the religious order; the Church's infallibility has neither the purpose nor the effect of putting an end to that process, but of regulating it, to prevent it from going astray, from losing its way. The Church neither teaches nor

---

* Sabatier, *Op. Cit.*, 327.

holds that there has been no evolution within her since her beginning, in her organization, her doctrine, or her practices; but she holds that that evolution has been legitimate within the order, logic, and vital necessity of her first institution so that, despite all such changes or rather by those very changes, she has kept the Gospel alive, she has remained that Gospel. The Church neither teaches nor holds that the world and men, dogma and faith, Christian religion and evangelical morality exist only to exalt her own authority, but regards herself as the providential and indispensable instrument of the preservation, propagation, and fulfillment of the Gospel on earth; her avowed and not at all vain pretension which her actions justify is to be an ecumenical service of salvation, not a universal tyranny over souls.

It must be admitted—and this is if not an excuse then at least a partial explanation for the adverse judgments aimed at Catholicism by the distinguished scholars who are unfamiliar with it in the intimate reality of its spirit and its work—it must be admitted, we repeat, that the humanly inevitable danger for a religious power as strongly constituted and as constantly menaced as the Catholic Church would be to confuse fidelity to the tradition with immobility within the tradition, the preservation of the faith with the maintenance of the formulary and of lethargy of mind in respect of the object of belief, the legitimacy of what exists today with the absolute identity of past with present, the interests of religion with the temporal advantages of the hierarchy. This danger, which certainly exists for the Catholic Church, has in certain circumstances seemed extremely threatening, has indeed not always been averted on all points and in every particular case. The marvel is that, taken all in all, the Roman Church has in the main escaped it; she has always taken herself in hand and reformed in time; she has not, like the Greek Church, unconsciously allowed herself to be brought to a standstill; despite conservative tendencies which seemed to demand only to be taken to excess, despite a discipline which, seen from the outside, looked as if it must lead to intellectual sterility, despite the temptation inherent in all absolute power to neglect or to suppress the rights of the individual, she has not ceased to be an institution truly alive and Christian, a minister of truth and of charity, a school of virtue and at the same time respect, the seat of a fertile development of Christianity and of religious thought. The point is that Catholicism, like the Gospel of which it is both sequel and permanent expression, has never been totally realized at any given historical moment, and that it is constantly in the process of being realized in the work it accomplishes on earth by an ever more extended and more varied application of its principle. The many different imperfections which one notices are the stuff of the progress which it is preparing to accomplish, and the repugnance which it rarely fails to register with regard to all the changes which take place around it, is in proportion to the effort it is already engaged in making to accommodate them.

Jesus and the Gospel are always alive in the Church, whatever may be said on this subject by the Doctors of individualist Christianity; as their critique of Catholicism takes up half their thesis, we have been obliged to respond to it in a general fashion, without denying ourselves the possibility of reconsidering the question in detail at a later date. What have they to put in place of the Catholic Church, and what is it they want to substitute for the tottering edifice of the old reformed confessions? The principle of salvation by faith, whatever the belief. We have no compunction in saying: try it; it will be interesting to hear you give an account of your faith if you take care to add, according to your conviction, that your belief is immaterial to salvation. This wholly new principle may well prove difficult to apply; it is too narrow and elusive a perch on which to seat a religion; but as a principle of religious anarchy it leaves little to be desired. Opposition to Catholicism and infinite division: this is individualist Christianity, and it will never be anything but Protestantism.

The Definition of Religion

If one is to believe the relatively moderate critics to whom we are indebted for the most recent works of importance on the history of Christian dogma and the philosophy of religion, the essence of religion is to be found in religious experience [sentiment] and true religion is religious experience in its purest form, such as was felt by Jesus, and as may be experienced by his disciples after his example. "Christianity," says Mr. Harnack,* "is that religion in which the faculty of leading a happy and holy life is associated with faith in God as the Father of Jesus Christ." By that he intends to convey that the object of the Christian religion is to bring the human conscience into a state of peace and holiness through the feeling [sentiment] of filial trust in God which Jesus demonstrates in the Gospel with respect to his Heavenly Father. This is the whole of religion; this is perfect religion. Thus understood, even the very idea of religion becomes indistinguishable from revelation; for revelation is no longer conceived as a supernatural manifestation of truths grasped by the human intellect; it is merely the sense of the divine, religious experience considered in relation to its object which is God; seen in the context of its subject this sentiment is called religion, and looked at from the point of view of its content—trust in God the Father, or the God who is the object of this trust—it is called revelation. Revelation therefore excludes all the word in itself means in normal usage: the communication of a truth; in the matter of religion the communication of truths concerning salvation. Would it not have been prudent, in the interests of avoiding ambiguity, to leave the term revelation to the theologians, who still reserve a special meaning for this ancient word to which they have acquired an inalienable right? The confusion is even more unfortunate in that religion and revelation are distinct notions, both of them real and, moreover, closely associated and relating to the same object, since all positive religions have been thought of in one way or another as divine revelations, but revelations of a definite object, not merely the imprint of the divine on the human soul.

* *Dogmengeschichte* (*Grundriss*, 3rd ed., vol. 1).

I

For the common run of theologians and even for ordinary folk, the term religious revelation means revealed religion. Thus, before defining revelation, one should have some notion of religion. What is religion? Mr. Sabatier tells us that "it is a conscious, voluntary relationship, entered into by the distressed soul, with the mysterious power on which the soul feels that it and its fate depend. This communion with God takes place through prayer."* The words "relationship" and "communion" should not be allowed to impair the purely subjective character of the religion with which we are concerned, for Mr. Sabatier's God is "entirely interior,"[†] and the revelation of God is already "in the prayer itself."[‡] The definition offered us is evidently taken neither from history nor from the present constitution of religions; it is a psychological explanation of their origin which has been made into a definition of religion itself and presented as the ideal type to which all religion must conform and to which Christianity must be reduced. This definition expresses, to a nicety, what religion essentially is for the individual; but, in so doing, it settles, even before it begins to address, an extremely important question which neither the history of religions nor religious psychology will let us neglect, and this is, whether religion is something purely individual and subjective, or whether it is not rather, at the same time as being an indefinite series of psychological phenomena, an objective and consistent reality, an institution of salvation, the highest form of human sociability. Such a question cannot be resolved a priori or in the name of an entirely personal experience which may quite well be incomplete. The experience of the centuries also has a right to make itself heard, and the universal witness of humanity throughout all ages must be admitted as evidence in a debate which is of equal interest to all men. As no living religion has yet come into being in a purely spiritual and personal fashion, anyone may, with good reason, contest the right of the learned proponents of individualistic Christianity to make an arbitrary decision on the meaning of the word "religion" and to define as they will something with which the world has for so long been familiar.

In every age and everywhere, the idea of religion has referred directly to the worship of the divinity in the widest application of the phrase, and

---

* Sabatier, *Esquisse d'une philosophie de la religion*, 24.

† *Op. cit.*, 100.

‡ *Op. cit.*, 32.

not merely condensed in interior prayer, the "movement of the soul making contact with the mysterious power whose presence it feels, even before
being able to give it a name." It is true that in the absence of such prayer
there is no religion in the individual, whatever homage may seem to be
rendered to God by the mechanical recitation of liturgical formulas; but, if
one retains the ordinary sense of the words and pays due respect to the
nature of things, one will not contend that "wherever this prayer wells up
and moves the soul, even in the absence of any form or any established
doctrine, there is living religion."* In order to accept this last assertion,
would one not first of all need to know whether religion has ever come into
being without any form whatsoever and without any kind of idea of the one
who is being adored? The movement of the soul which is presented as the
whole of religion cannot be anything more than its principle in the
individual, its psychological root in humanity; but religion itself is something
more akin to the complete development of this movement, the expression
deemed suitable and obligatory for all human individuals, the identical sen-
timents which all must experience in relation to God. For man has always
considered religion to be something objective and collective; as the means
by which a group of human beings or the whole of humanity might communicate with the divinity, have efficacious recourse to his protection and
become the recipients of his support. The bond which binds the divinity to
his worshipers, and which associates the latter with each other in communion with that same God, is a spiritual and invisible one at base, even
though it may sometimes have been conceived through images which are
material enough; but whatever the idea may be and however pure it may
have become, at least there is an idea, a symbolic form of belief which is
not considered arbitrary, and rites which may be said to carry within them
and effect the divine communion they signify. Our modern psychologists
may find this manner of understanding religion too crude. It is the one
which is to be found in all religions, even Protestantism; what they are
calling religion is not what poor humanity has understood by it up to
the present. They would have done well to leave the word "religion" too
to the common run of humanity and invent a new word for a new thing,
for the thing they regard as the religion of the future and which is not their
own religion now because they officially belong to a system of worship
which is not that pure religion and has no desire to be so.

Religion, as it exists and has always existed, is inconceivable without
the symbols and rites through which the religious life common to the

* *Loc. cit.*

adepts of the same system of worship is assumed to be described, created, maintained, and developed. Of religion's constitutive elements the most perceptible and the most obviously consistent is the rite. The rite exists by reason of religious belief, and this also explains it. Religious morality is also an element of religion. Beliefs and morals do not occur to the same extent in all religions; but no religion is entirely without them. Worship always has an object. Man does not commend himself to a power of which his mind has not formed some notion. Nor does he believe that divine protection will be granted him without some corresponding obligation, nor that his mode of being and behaving in the ordinary course of his life is totally without effect on his relations with the divinity. Religious doctrine and morals may be different, they vary from one religion to another; they can fail, they do not persist without change even in a single religion; yet no religion exists without religious ideas and religious duties. One cannot say that these ideas and duties are not part of the religion, for, without religious beliefs and religious duties, religion would not exist at all. In the order of logic, if not in the order of reality, the religious idea precedes religious experience [sentiment] and both come before religious duties and rites. In fact, all these elements support and complement each other, combining to make up what everyone calls religion, that is, the worship accorded to the divinity by man as an individual and as a member of human society: worship which is the internal and external expression of his belief and of his feelings [sentiments], which is supposed to put him in communication with the divine world, which, in a more or less perfect fashion, endows his moral life with a principle, a rule, a support, and a purpose.

Thus understood, and notwithstanding the particular and defective forms it has taken outside Israelite monotheism and Christianity, religion is not a debased manifestation or corruption of the pure system of worship which Protestant criticism has always thought to discover but never actually realized. In the last analysis it is certain that religion is based on man's experience of his absolute dependence in relation to God and on the trust he places in this God on whom he absolutely depends. But just as science is based on the sense of curiosity aroused in man by his perception of things, and on the trust he places either in the reality of his perceptions or in the reality of their object, and yet science consists neither in the faculty of knowing nor in the need to know with certitude, nor even in the general notion of being and of truth, together with the mind's attachment to this abstract idea; and just as virtue is founded on the sentiment and perception of moral good and on the faculty of willing it, and yet consists neither in the simple discernment of good and the simple power for good, nor even in the general notion of duty and the general will to perform it; so religion is founded on religious experience yet does not consist uniquely in this experience, nor even in a general disposition of submission and trust in relation to the divinity. As science consists essentially in the knowledge of things, and moral perfection in the accomplishment of good, so religion consists in a certain realization of the divine. This realization will be incomplete, relative, symbolic. But science too is incomplete, relative, symbolic, and no one, for that reason, reduces it to an individual, psychological principle. To sweep away all its given facts on the pretext that the principle of knowledge is alone unsusceptible to change would rightly be considered absurd; to oblige each individual to reconstruct by his own efforts and for his own personal use the entire body of knowledge which he may need would be to condemn science to a swift demise and far indeed from favoring its advance. Like science, human morality is incomplete; it is, like science too, relative in certain respects, and always perfectible: however, one would not attempt to limit it uniquely to the power of doing good and the taste for it. To do away with morality, pleading that everyone holds it in its entirety within themselves, will never be other than a dangerous utopia, and to expect each person to discover in himself, by his own means, the rules of practice for all his duties would be to condemn humanity to barbarity. Science lives in its imperfect results. Morality lives in acts of virtue which constantly fall short of the ideal it pursues. Science does not set forth the absolute truth; moral action does not set forth the absolute good; yet both science and virtue subsist no less as something real between the human faculties which produce them and the infinite object which they strive to attain. Although science and virtue are only alive in individuals, the tradition of one, as of the other, persists outside the individuals who participate in them, if one takes each one separately, and it is certain that the science and morals of the individuals would not amount to much without the help of this tradition which they have appropriated for themselves, and which has a kind of impersonal existence in its formulas and in its rules, in the common level of intellectual and moral culture, and which is made to bear fruit for everyone through teaching and education. Just as science can neither exist nor subsist without the doctrines and formulas which remain in the keeping of its learned men, nor morality without the precepts which are preserved in society with the concurrence of good people, religion can neither exist nor subsist without beliefs or without traditional rites, maintained and kept by pious men. It is something real and solid between the sense of the divine in man and the God who is beyond man's embrace.

The necessity of symbol and rite as expressions of beliefs and of the religious system of worship, as vehicle, safeguard, condition of a living religion, is founded on the nature of the two terms united by religion, on the nature of man and that of God. In order to understand how learned and not irreligious men could have imagined religion as completely realized in the individual, notwithstanding all positive belief and all external manifestation, one needs to recall the total force of rationalist prejudice against whatever is not the object of science or scientific demonstration, and the intensity of the Protestant prejudice against an external system of worship, prejudices which are condemned, the one by healthy philosophy and the other by the religious experience of all ages. And yet these learned men, so contemptuous of symbols and rites, have no intention of doing without symbols and rites. They will make their symbols as abstract as possible and their rites as cold as may be. They will then have succeeded in reducing their religious efficacy; they could not eliminate them entirely without completely eliminating religion. "Piety," writes Mr. Sabatier, "is only conscious in ourselves and discernible to others when incarnate in its intellectual expression or image. A religion without doctrine, a piety without thought, a feeling [sentiment] without expression are things which are essentially contradictory. It is as vain to want to grasp pure piety (and yet is this not what Mr. Sabatier has tried to do?) as to seek to define the thing in itself in philosophy."* One could not have put it better nor more palpably demonstrated the inadequacy of the definition given by Mr. Sabatier himself, which includes almost none of the real or permanent elements of religion, of what it has been, of what it continues to be in the world: belief and worship, homage rendered to God by human society rather than by each human individual alone. Should one have refrained from encumbering religion with beliefs in order to avoid the nuisance of dogmas, and from mentioning first of all the essentially social character of religion, in order to be more certain of eliminating the Church?

On the contrary, it is necessary to insist on the social character from which religion draws its strength and which is the guarantee of its survival. Man is aware of depending on God as an individual; he also knows that he depends on him as a member of human society and with the human society to which he belongs. It is all men who by the same right depend

---

* *Op. cit.*, 404–405.

on God collectively, one might almost say in solidarity; not the individual abstracted from his actual life and concentrated in the most secret intimacy of his heart, but the whole man, just as he lives and behaves in the precise situation dictated by his relations with his family and with society. If all religions present themselves to us in social guise this can only be by virtue of a natural necessity, a deep-seated logic even more significant for the historian and the philosopher because unpremeditated. Both reason and history force us to include the character of a social institution in the definition of religion. The form of this institution has varied, like the beliefs and rites, with the beliefs and the rites and from one religion to another and also in the course of the historical development of the same religion; but all religions, even the most imperfect, have been and are in some manner religious institutions. The crudest cults appear to consist almost exclusively of traditional rituals, so rudimentary and vague does their belief, the intellectual form of the religion, appear to us, but at least they have the element of a common rite, generally accepted as efficacious and indispensable forever. In most of the ancient religions the rite did not cease to predominate over belief and to be the most stable element of religious tradition; yet with the growth of civilization the myths which were bound up with the liturgical action have taken increasingly fixed even if never definitive forms and have even succeeded in becoming susceptible to philosophical interpretation. The priesthood, under different guises, appears everywhere in the role of guardian of religious tradition, and it may be said that tradition itself is a constitutive element of religion. This necessity for religious tradition is founded on the social nature of religion: our ancestors were in the same relation to the divinity as are men today, and the religious society which they formed—leaving aside the fact that we do not think of it as totally dissolved by death as far as they are concerned—is maintained under exactly the same conditions through their descendants or through those who adhere to the same faith.

II

This simple description of religion, for it is not, strictly speaking, a definition, is sufficient to refute certain hypotheses which belong to popular rationalism and which the theologians of individualism are no more inclined to admit than we are. It is clear that religion is not a system of superstitious practices invented by priests or by the original leaders of the people in order to strengthen their authority over the ignorant masses. Religions without a distinctive priesthood were known to antiquity, and religion has always predated official priesthoods. From the most ancient times one finds the head of the family, the tribal chief, and finally the king presiding over the sacrifices and acts of public worship by virtue of some sort of natural designation which rules out the least suspicion of deceit. The more or less dubious role of the magician is not to be confused with that of the priest, and, as a rule, the magician himself has always been the first dupe of his enchantments. The most rudimentary forms of religion, spirit worship, ancestor worship, and fetishism, are not the result of someone's deliberate deceit but spring rather from a simple ignorance shared by everyone. It was not that the most astute succeeded in touching the imagination of his fellows by a confident show of illusions; it was that they found themselves unable to arrive at any worthier representation of the divinity without whom they were unable to live. Before long, tradition endowed the most singular practices with a sacred character, and the spontaneity of the superstition made the fraud itself an unconscious one. "It is not the priesthood which explains religion, it is religion which explains the priesthood."* The necessity for the priesthood arises from religion's social character. The limitation of religious office to particular families or to a certain caste, which was the most usual form of the priesthood in ancient times, presupposes a certain degree of civilization and social development; it seems to have been less a case of bands of priests employing a tissue of inventions in order to play on the superstitious veneration of their fellows, than the societies themselves delegating the common religious obligation, which is to say that of public worship, to a certain number of people who thus accepted the responsibility, honor, and profit of that delegation.

Nor is religion a childish explanation of the world. All religions, of whatever sort, are something other than speculative theories or cosmological hypotheses. To this there are no exceptions save in the case of the natural religion of rationalist spiritualism, which is a philosophical system and not a real religion. All religions which exist or have existed were systems of worship before they were cosmogonies. The myths of cosmogony are initial attempts by the reflective mind to explain the world by reference to the gods; but the gods were not invented to explain the world. To find God, neither the unschooled man, nor indeed the scholar, finds it necessary to

---

* *Op. cit.*, 8.

refer to the problem of the creation; he senses God, if one may so express it, before he proves his existence, and he fears him as absolute master before he recognizes him as the author of all things. God did not begin as the explanation of nature: he is the force hidden in nature before which man feels himself both helpless and ecstatic and to which, by a spontaneous movement of his being, he feels the need to entrust himself. Man did not believe in spirits of the storm and of the waters, of life and of death, in order to understand lightning, tempests, the movement of the tides, vegetation, animal life, diseases, his own origin and destiny. He as it were glimpsed the spirit in the phenomenon which declared it to him, and was filled with fear and hope before it. Religion did not spring fully formed from the human intelligence, but rather from the human heart, from man's awareness of his own weakness before the infinite power which revealed itself to him in things. "The question man is asking in religion," observes Mr. Sabatier, "is never other than the question of salvation, and if in asking it he seems sometimes to be pursuing the enigma of the universe, it is only in order to pursue the enigma of his life."* One could go further and say that there was no question, since the response appeared spontaneously and the problem did not present itself clearly to the intellect as susceptible of more than one solution. Religion proceeds from a state of prostration and a desire in some fashion infinite. It is not that the desire proceeds from "faith in life" alone, nor that it is no more than a "superior form" of "the instinct of self-preservation." The very experience which reveals to man the force hidden in things does not fail to show him the goodness which hides with that force. If religion is born of fear and hope, it is nonetheless not born of a fear which comes only from the outside, nor of a hope springing only from within as an instinctive reaction to the depressive effect of fear. Hope, like fear, has its own foundation, and nature which is well-equipped to frighten man is also well-equipped to reassure him. It may perhaps have been in picturing this sentiment of trust, which is the vital element of religion, as entirely spontaneous that one has thought religion itself to be entirely psychological, entirely individual, pure sentiment from its first origin. Yet it is clear that trust, like fear, was the result of a very simple perception in a being capable of feeling his own helplessness and of aspiring to his own reinstatement.

At this point it should be pointed out that, in supposing there to be an active spirit behind every natural phenomenon, the men of former times

* *Op. cit.*, 13.

were no more mistaken than those who acknowledge the existence of a supreme cause in the universe, who conceive it to be intelligent and free, who see the impossibility of a continuous series of contingent effects without a first and necessary cause, a series which would represent the movement, devoid of both a point of departure and a goal, of a world without reason to exist, fatally proceeding toward an end dictated by chance. They were mistaken in attributing a separate cause to each phenomenon, a spirit which was the phenomenon personified. Yet their error was not the ultimate anchor of their religious faith, and the feelings they experienced with respect to their gods did not result from the ideas they entertained about spirits. They were capable of absolute trust in a genius which, for our theology, would represent no more than an entirely subordinate power. This type of separation between religious thought and religious experience is not found solely at the lower levels of religion. Is it not true that the purely rational proofs of the existence of God are not the sufficient principle of our faith in him; that the metaphysical notion of a Supreme Being is not the immediate source of our piety; that our idea of God, absolute as it may seem to us, is still, by its very nature, a grandiose anthropomorphism, and that the true God is the being whom that notion represents but fails entirely to express, which is to say the living God before whom man is conscious of his nothingness and his wretchedness, in whom he takes refuge as if in the source of all the good things of which he stands in need? And in this sense might one not say that it is not the God of religion who has changed so greatly but the ideas through which human intelligence has striven to conceive him?

The universal character of religion is proof of its substantial reality, its fundamental truth. Religion is as essential to man as reason or the consciousness of duty. It is of little consequence that there have been so many defective religions and some irreligious men, nor even that no religion has failed to give men occasion for certain abuses. Man has been intelligent ever since he has been man, and has fallen and each day falls once again into errors as numberless as the stars of the sky or the grains of sand on the seashore: does it therefore follow that truth does not exist and that man is in no way aware of it? Errors prove nothing against the truth, for, if there were no truth there would be no errors; the existence of fools proves nothing against reason, for, if there were no reason there would be no fools either. Man was capable of morality and virtue from the beginning, and from the beginning man has been a sinner, vicious even: does it therefore follow that virtue is no more than a word, or that man is forever and absolutely incapable of reaching it? Vice and sin prove nothing against duty, for, if there were no duty there would be neither vice nor sin; the existence of vicious men proves nothing against human morality, for, if there were neither a moral faculty nor a moral law in humanity, there would be no vicious men either. False religions are, in their order, what ignorance or secular errors are in the intellectual order, hereditary vices in the moral order. Ignorance and error do not entirely blot out reason and truth in man; vice does not entirely destroy morality in him; superstition does not absolutely deprive him of religion. Atheists who really are atheists are no more than a tiny exception in the whole ensemble of humanity; they are above all skeptics, those whom the Scriptures refer to as "the scornful," who ridicule everything, including themselves. They are few enough to be counted. If this exception proved anything against religion, it would count in the same way against the reality of the true and the good, for these delicate and subtle minds have thought, by doubting, to set themselves above reason, morality, and religion: they have succeeded only in setting themselves outside these and outside real humanity which lives without "losing itself in its thoughts." Atheism of the crude, violent, and noisy variety only too frequent in our time is made up half from the desire that God should not exist and half from the fear that he really does exist: this rebellion against religion witnesses to its force and not to its nonexistence. To some, one may apply Mr. Sabatier's remark: "A man who claims to be an atheist is never such except in respect of the God of other people."* For it is this idea of God which the atheist most frequently rejects, confusing it with its actual object which he thinks he is rejecting and which he fails to understand. Yet if this negation does not make him into an atheist as absolute as he imagines himself to be, it nonetheless situates him off the path on which man finds the perfect light of life and true happiness of the soul. Mr. Sabatier opens the doors of his church too wide when he lets them admit as God's friends all those generous souls who serve "Justice" and "Goodness," all the philosophers and scholars who seek "Truth," all the artists who adore "Beauty." Giving abstractions capital letters does not suffice to identify them with God, nor is having an ideal sufficient to admit one to a religion. The best one can say in favor of those who have no other cult than that of justice, goodness, truth, beauty, is that through them they may to a greater or lesser extent draw near to the kingdom of heaven, unconsciously and at times with their backs turned to it. To enter there it is necessary to have suffered, understood, and lived infinite terror and infinite hope. In spite of these exceptions, it may be said that all men are religious, and that this they are, not by an extraordinary effort of mind, nor by a violent and fantastic leap of the will: for if an abnormal tension of the human faculties were required to

* Op. cit., 28.

place man within religion it would be the religious men and not the atheists who would form the exception. Men are religious because they have an instinct for religion, an innate respect for God, and an innate need to put their trust in him.

This religious instinct is not an isolated faculty, unconnected to the higher powers of our soul, able quite on its own, by a sort of mystic intuition, to resolve the problem of life. The proponents of individualism are true to their own logic in seeing in its manifestations nothing more than "the fortunate interior crisis through which human life transforms itself and opens a way through to the ideal life";* but they seem to be too forgetful of the part played by the intellect, moral conscience, and will in bringing this interior crisis to a happy conclusion. The religious instinct is closely associated with these master faculties; it has a hand in their exercise, and they help it to find its object. As a faculty, our intelligence is the power and the need we have of knowing things, and the reasons for things, by going back to the proximate causes and then to the remote causes of our impressions. In humanity this power is never exhausted and this need never fully satisfied: they cannot be so because, the sharper they become and the more they witness their own operations, the more evident it becomes that the intellect has an immediate grasp only of the image of things, an impression of reality, the special relation in which man finds himself to the universe which surrounds him; that it does not really know either man or the universe in themselves, and that at bottom and beyond all things lies Infinity, the absolute reality and truth which escape it. By this route the reason leads to God as to the mystery which explains all, the incomprehensible through which all knowledge is justified; it may even be said to seek and demand it, to seek it unconsciously, to demand it involuntarily. Man has the sense and faculty of the good; but the appetite for the good is no more satisfied in him than the appetite for the true, and his will proves in practice less sufficient than his reason: the good attracts and transcends us; it even judges us and condemns us, as if we could will or at least desire a perfection we are unable to realize, as if this perfection retreated before us in proportion to the efforts we make to reach it, our activity being spent sometimes in pursuing it, often in abandoning it, always in mourning for it, without at any time possessing it in its fullness. By this route too the conscience leads to God as to the perfection which is inaccessible and yet which may be emulated, as

---

* *Op. cit.*, 23.

to the justice which commands and brooks no argument, the good which enraptures without surrendering itself; the conscience too may be said to seek God and demand him, to seek him as ruler and as support, to demand him as recompense; but to seek is not to find, to demand is not to possess. That which casts man at the feet of God, that which prompts the intelligence to see him and the conscience to call upon him, is the consciousness [sentiment] of universal poverty which is apparent not only in the highest faculties, but in the whole order of human life, in the physical no less than the moral order, and which makes it somehow necessary for man in his wretchedness to attach himself to and actively to affirm the infinite power which he apprehends as existing at the root of everything, which he needs to know as a source of assistance and which, in the simplicity of his trust, he does find to be such, and thanks to which he in some way takes possession of himself, develops a moral force of which he was previously unaware, and becomes better in proportion to his trust. One could say with equal truth that the better he becomes, the more he trusts himself to it, for faith results much less from argument than from experience, man's experience of his own weakness when he looks only to himself, and his experience of his strength when he relies on God. The forms taken by this experience have varied; some of them now seem to us crude because they are no longer sufficient for us. At the root of everything there is, as an incitement to faith, man's innate instinct to seek, in his wretchedness, an invincible protector; this protector he is shown in the infinite power which his intelligence perceives behind the movement of this world; however, he does not attach himself to it definitively except by the actual practice of a trust which he certainly feels to be a duty, where he finds, in spite of a thousand apparent disappointments, the divine assistance which strengthens him in the face of his present difficulties and his anxieties for the future. It is thus that the religious instinct comes to the aid of the intellect and the conscience, that the will is invited to find its point of attachment beyond itself, and that through the combined effect of all his powers man attains to God.

Religion perfects man's religious sense just as science perfects his reason and virtue his will; that is not to say that it perfects it by filling it to overflowing but rather by stimulating it and lifting it more and more toward its object which continually eludes a definitive embrace, as if the period of this present life were meant only to be an effort toward God, and because it is, in reality, nothing else. For the whole human soul tends toward God, absolute truth, perfect justice, almighty goodness, infinite reality; it tends toward him not in order to lose itself in him, but to find itself there eternally. To deny God and religion is therefore to deny man himself, to make of him a living contradiction, a desire so immense that I am at a loss to describe it, opening upon nothingness. Since man has an infinite desire for truth, for justice, for life, they therefore exist to infinity, in God, and man truly reaches God through religion, as he truly tends toward him through the orientation of his spiritual activity, intellect, and will; and because he knows that in religion he acquires, or one might almost say makes, truth, justice, and life, man believes and lifts himself up by faith, not in an isolated fashion by shutting himself up in his own conscience, but with his brothers, using their society to help him and helping them through his own, placing his reliance in religious tradition and realizing it afresh in himself. God is the necessary postulate of human activity, in the order of the intellect as primary cause and absolute truth, in the moral order as master and supreme judge, in the order of religion, which includes the entire conscious life of man, as sovereign and beneficent protector. If God were not and if religion were no more than a dream, man himself would be a mere illusion lost in the void.

But if religion is a reality, its symbols are not in vain nor its rites powerless. It is true that religious formulas do not constitute religion any more than scientific formulas are science. Yet scientific formulas contain and transmit science; in the same way religious symbols contain and perpetuate faith. One may correct and improve those symbols, as they may also be changed; one can never do without them. They are not God, that is, the absolute truth incomprehensible to us, but they are his image and representation: one cannot imagine or represent him without them. They are the relative expression through which we glimpse the impenetrable Eternal. Nor are rites in themselves religion; but in a certain fashion they too contain religious life and communicate it. Their efficacy, like that of formulas, relates to the meaning attached to them; but man can no more do without religious rites than he can prevent himself from attaching a meaning to them. Whatever their mode of action, these rites are certainly active in all religions, and without being the religious life, they maintain it; without being God himself, they make him felt and convey him. In the same way the institutions which shelter religion, the diverse forms taken by religious tradition, while not by themselves religion, participate in its divine reality and in its necessity to the extent to which they guarantee the preservation, propagation, and progress of religion among men. Without these aids man would not encounter God and religion at the root of his being; and once he has met them there, he needs the same assistance to retain them.

The Idea of Revelation

In asserting that revelation was not "a communication once and for all of unchangeable doctrines which simply have to be kept securely in mind,"* Mr. Sabatier intended to contradict at one and the same time the ideas of revelation held by orthodox Protestants and by Catholics. This, indeed, is the revelation orthodox Protestantism would find necessary for its own defense. But it is not the idea upon which Catholicism is founded. Although a number of us use a terminology which is fairly consistent with conservative Protestant opinion, if the suggested definition is to correspond more or less to the Catholic notion of revelation, the "unchangeable doctrines" will have to be replaced by "certain truths" and the words "kept securely in mind" by "exploited and developed." Against the definition he believes to be traditional and untenable and which although perhaps untrue is also not truly traditional, Mr. Sabatier sets up a new conception which consists of seeing in revelation "the creation, the refinement, the progressive clarity of the consciousness of God in man as an individual and in humanity."† Clearly this definition, like the same author's definition of religion, errs less by what it says than by what it fails to say. In it, revelation, like religion itself, appears to be reduced to a psychological phenomenon, "the consciousness of God in man" being no more than this; and it seems that "the creation, the refinement, the progressive clarity" in question are not precisely the knowledge of God in man inasmuch as God might be the absolute source, inexhaustible object and supreme end of revelation, but an entirely human process deemed to encompass its own principle and end and itself to embrace the totality of its object, so that God revealed would be nothing else than humanity's religious consciousness or the movement of this consciousness.

Now although, on the one hand, when looked at in man, revelation is man's consciousness of God, not God's consciousness of himself in man (Mr. Sabatier's definition might, without too much difficulty, be interpreted

---

* A. Sabatier, *Esquisse d'une philosophie de la religion*, 34–35.
† *Op. cit.*, 34.

in this sense without perhaps straying so very far from his thought), on the other hand, considered in itself, in its cause, and in its object, revelation is neither more nor less than God's manifestation to man. Although taking place in man and, like God himself, immanent to man, this manifestation always transcends man by virtue of its origin, content, and destination.

I

Where revelation is at issue, "doctrine" must not be confused with "truth." Accustomed as we are to look at the faith objectively and theoretically as a system of propositions rigorously formulated and divinely sanctioned, we have difficulty in conceiving a religion without precise dogma, a revelation without an official creed. On this point, the habits of mind which have been imparted to us by Scholasticism must be set right by the facts of history. If a profession of faith, officially established and regarded as immutable, were essential to the constitution of a religion, only Christianity, from the end of the apostolic period, with its traditional creed, would succeed in being a religion, yet still with the proviso that the immutability should not be understood in a fashion so concrete as to exclude any real development of the original creed. A certain form of belief is indispensable to all religion, but absolute rigidity in belief must be excluded from all religion, being impossible to achieve and against the nature of man in whom religion has its home. The ancient pagan cults had religious beliefs but neither absolute dogmas nor compulsory confessions of faith; these they were probably incapable of producing until they had brought some sort of criticism to bear on their faith, and as long as they were without any common philosophy whose notions they could have applied to their religion. Even Israelite monotheism and primitive Christianity, whose belief was so pure and firm, did not have a dogmatic creed if that be taken to mean a series of articles of faith designated as the subject matter of teaching and the definitive expression of the belief. The prophets believed and taught that Yahweh, God of Israel, was the only God, and proclaimed his future reign. In order to translate this belief into a formula appropriate to our theological point of view, we should make a creed consisting of three articles: Yahweh alone is God; Yahweh God is the God of Israel; Yahweh God will save Israel and will be glorified in her in the sight of all men. But if the two first points are clearly affirmed in the Old Testament, the third is always subject to variation, and the idea of a doctrinal summary which might have acted as a rule of faith occurred neither to Moses nor to the prophets. The only imperative article in which the Law and the Prophets are summarized is not, properly speaking, a dogmatic statement but a moral precept: you shall serve Yahweh God alone, God of the universe, who is our God. The duty to believe is not thought to require proof, and the belief itself is adjudged sufficiently clear to the eye of faith, without any further explication or definition. Judaism today still does without an official creed and has not for that reason ceased to be a religion. As for the Christianity of the first century, even though the work of reflection from which Christological dogma was to emerge may have been sketched out in the New Testament, neither the gospels nor the rest of the apostolic writings contain a didactic account of the things one must believe in order to be a Christian. Jews, who already believe in God, were baptized in the name of Jesus Christ, Son of God, as soon as they acknowledged him in this quality. Pagans had first to declare their belief in the one and only God, Father almighty, who made heaven and earth and, as the baptism was a spiritual one, accompanied by the gift of the Holy Spirit, all those converted were before long baptized in the name of the Father, the Son, and the Holy Spirit.* This baptismal profession of faith was not originally proposed as a formal subscription by the intellect to three doctrinal theses: the creation of the world by the Father, the salvation of men by the Son, the sanctification of the Church by the Holy Spirit; nor to a metaphysical commentary on the baptismal rite on the theme of the unity of God in three distinct persons. It was, first of all, the consecration of the candidate to the God to whom Jesus reconciled him, to whom the Spirit was to unite him. The terms of this consecration implied a threefold assertion of faith in the creator God, Jesus the Savior, and the sanctifying Spirit, without any theoretical explanation of creation, salvation, or grace. This explanation, which is the effect of the operation of Christian thought on the assertion of faith, constitutes, properly speaking, theological doctrine, and when this doctrine is officially sanctioned by the Church it becomes dogma. It may therefore be said, in general, that the Israelite religion and apostolic Christianity relied on assertions of faith rather than doctrines and dogmas in the strict sense, the assertions of faith enclosing at least the seed of the truths which were later interpreted and developed in dogma.†

---

* On this question, see Hurter, *Theologiae dogmaticae compendium*, vol. 3, th. 209.

† "Dogma is a truth of the faith proposed by the Church in an authentic doctrinal judgment." P. de la Barre, *La vie du dogme catholique* [Paris: Lethielleux, 1898]. In this definition can be recognized the threefold distinction of the truth of the faith, theological doctrine and dogmatic definition. It is quite common to call a truth of the faith a dogma and thus to speak, for example, of the dogmas contained in the Scriptures. If we have avoided using the term dogma in its wider sense here, it is because it tends to give rise to confusion from a historical point of view rather than because of any difference of authority between the simple truth of the faith and the dogma. In the dogma defined by the Church the truth of the faith subsists under a new form with an authority just as great as in the initial assertion.

This being said, it is easy to understand how the proper and direct object of revelation should be the simple truths contained in the assertions of the faith, not the doctrines and the dogmas as such: doctrines and dogmas are referred to as revealed because the revealed truths inhabit the authorized explanations which are the Church's doctrines and dogmas. Even the notion of the incarnate Word, in the fourth gospel, is no exception to the rule, for it appears as an assertion of faith, not as a theory of the Word and the Incarnation. Thus the history of revelation invites us to refrain from seeing as the essential and indispensable element of this revelation the purely intellectual knowledge of theoretical, abstract propositions supposed to be the direct objects of divine communication, subsequently to be handed down from generation to generation like a ready-made lesson in which nothing may ever be altered for any reason whatsoever. The truths of revelation are alive in the assertions of faith before being analyzed in the speculations of doctrine; their native form is a supernatural intuition and affirmation of faith, not an abstract consideration and systematic definition of their object. It must be added, indeed, that even though revelation is now preserved in ecclesiastical doctrine and dogma, the economy of faith has not been altered; for it is always as assertions of faith that doctrine and dogma serve as foundation for the Christian life; as doctrinal theory or dogmatic theology they serve rather to maintain the harmony of religious belief with humanity's scientific development.

Yet it is equally true, and has already been established, that there is of necessity an intellectual element in religious faith, or at the very least a rational image of the God feared and desired by the soul. As soon as faith is obliged to live and increase within the realm of philosophy and learning, this intellectual element, which faith uses as a support, will produce dogma, because the religious concept of the universe, and of man and life, demands to be brought into harmony with the scientific knowledge of those same objects. The most sincere believer could not be satisfied with an idea of God which failed to take in whatever knowledge about the world he himself possesses. The external forms of religious truth are bound, therefore, to adjust themselves upon contact with science, or the faith will be endangered. If the faith is to be kept secure, the religious idea, instead of allowing itself to be absorbed or dissolved by science, must seize on science and master it in order to put it to the service of faith. Theology, which springs directly from faith in contact with science, springs indirectly from revelation. As the term "revelation" is not, in normal usage, applied to objects of feeling or will, but to objects of knowledge, it is a term appropriate to true religion, seen in its intellectual aspect in the notions and discernments which God's supernatural action suggests to those whom he has particularly chosen to be the organs of his manifestation to humanity. These simple notions and discernments are not the effect of the purely rational operation of human thought on religious subjects. One has no right to set them outside the religion of which they are an integral and even essential part, since no religion is able to do without them. They are not of a scientific order, abstract and analytical, but appear intuitive, real, and synthetic. Although the reason recognizes and approves them, although it even provided the material for them, although, having perceived them and assimilated them, it may be able to analyze and coordinate them to a certain degree, they are not the fruit of reason alone. Divine revelation would be unintelligible to man if it did not adopt the form of a human concept; but this concept is not produced in man as the necessary result of his ratiocinations and research; it is offered him as symbol of the eternal truth which is infinitely beyond all created intelligence, and a light even beyond the symbol penetrates it in a certain fashion so as to render it divinely clear and efficacious.

It is very striking that all religions which have ever been, or now exist on earth, have always claimed to be revealed religions. The gods are everywhere supposed to have dictated the rules of their own system of worship; one does not call on them except by reason of having encountered them on one's path and become aware of their will. On the basis simply of the universal witness which guarantees the necessity and substantial truth of religion, one is bound to admit that religion is revelatory, not, to be sure, by virtue of some sort of absolute demand of human nature, but by virtue of a kind of positive law, in practice equivalent to such a necessity. Humanity, essentially religious, has no recollection of having created religion, but rather of having received and preserved it. Must we reject this witness because it is provided by all religions at once, and all religions cannot be true; or because, in the naive and antique form in which it has reached us, it is like a story told by children who have seen something new to them and are unable to describe it other than by metaphors as lively as they are unconscious, beneath which a person of mature years would discern a quite ordinary fact? The existence of false religions always bears witness in some manner to the truth of religion and consequently to that of revelation, the only historical form of religion. But the difficulty represented by the imperfection of the witness as such must be more closely examined.

II

The mythic concept of revelation was, we are told, common to all the peoples of antiquity: it consisted in discovering in everything celestial signs and the outward manifestation of divine secrets and the purposes of providence; even among the prophets of Israel, divine inspiration "is represented as a strange being invading the human being, like some kind of mental alienation or possession"; in Jesus the inspiration becomes purely interior and thereby "normal" because "religion and nature, the voice of God and the voice of conscience, the subject and the object of revelation, interpenetrate each other and become one"; theology shattered this beautiful harmony by making "the object of revelation" dogma, "that is to say, an intellectual concept," which meant "depriving it of its religious character by separating it from piety" and at the same time "bringing it into irremediable conflict with the reason which is always progressive"; to correct this fault in the Christian tradition, we are told, one need do no more than adopt a purely psychological idea of revelation and see "in all piety some positive manifestation of God," which makes revelation "evident, interior and progressive,"* and reestablishes religion on the unshakable foundation given it by Jesus. This unshakable foundation is what we already know, the religion of pure feeling, and it is neither the Christianity of Jesus nor even any religion at all. We know too that dogma, the assertion of faith, is essentially religious and, far from setting itself apart from piety, enters into it, and that, as doctrinal theory, its object is precisely to prevent conflicts between faith and reason rather than to make them inevitable. Therefore, what we have to do here is simply to establish the objective character of revelation, justify what is called "the mythological notion of revelation" in the prophets, and define the real idea of Christian revelation.

Because no religion is immutable and perfect to a point beyond perfection, no idea capable of encompassing God, and no formula adequate to express him, individualistic theologians imagine themselves entitled to strip all religions of their doctrinal content and to reduce all of them to the experience [sentiment] of the divine which would then comprise the one and only religion, true revelation. No religious belief would be revealed because the human soul senses God and does not see him. Religious thought would be like the reflection of religious experience in

* Sabatier, *op. cit.*, 36–61.

the intellect; but this image would not be divine. Moreover, the psychology of the new teachers tends to be somewhat uncertain and their theology rather elastic. It is hard to see clearly to what extent God is there, separate from the soul: it is almost as if the latter were the movement made by God in self-revelation, if indeed God himself might not be the image contemplated by the soul mirroring itself in its own thought. Not only would religion and revelation be two names for the same psychological phenomenon, but God and the soul would also be two names, of unequal proportion, to describe the same spiritual entity. However, if one prefers not to abandon both sound philosophy and the fundamental principle of religion at the same time, one is obliged to retain the essential distinction between God and man. Once this distinction is guaranteed, then from a causal point of view revelation in its most general sense will be the action of God, transcendent and immanent to the soul, on the soul itself; and, from the point of view of its effect, it will be the religious knowledge, entirely penetrated by the divine Spirit, which results from that action. The purely rational conclusions which, from his contemplation of the universe, man may draw by the use of his intellect alone, are not revelation. Even the facts or sensory impressions which anticipate or accompany revelation and serve as its vehicle, are no more than its customary occasions or normal conditions. So revelation does not consist simply of the impressions of respectful fear and filial trust which sum up religious sentiment. Why should one wish it to hide itself away in this obscure recess of the soul and remain estranged from the movement of thought which is the necessary accompaniment of a religious impression and which gives religious feeling [sentiment] its conscious form? Is not the idea of such a separation between the activity of our religious faculties and the fruit of their activity a contradiction in itself? If, too, the intention had been to provide religion with the absolute foundation it needed, is it not obvious that it was a mistake to look for this in man, and that religious feeling on its own provides no more solid a base than the contingent forms of religious thought, and that the absolute foundation of religion can exist in nothing human, but in God. If it is admitted that upon contact with the divine, there springs forth from the depths of the religious soul a lively light for the intelligence, communicable to other souls, then it is admitted that revelation is the production of a substantially divine truth, divinely initiated although always humanly perceived and formulated. Nothing more is needed in order to safeguard the truly traditional idea of revelation, nor will it follow that all religions were true in their own time or are so as regards their adherents, nor that one should categorize them all as revealed in themselves according to their degree of perfection.

Revelation does not exist as long as the truth revealed has not yet become intelligible to man or been, as it were, realized in him; yet it is no less true that it is offered to him as a divine teaching which he does not create but which is imposed upon him at the same time as it is manifested to him. To wish "that revelation might be as universal as religion itself, that it should spread as far downward and outward, rise to the same heights and be its constant accompaniment,"* is simply to deny the existence of error and abuse in religion. Neither error nor abuse can be a constituent part of true religion and divine revelation. To identify them with revelation is to make God responsible, or perhaps even a way of affirming that man is God and that God is man. There have been and still are false or debased religions, corrupt systems of worship. To say: "No form of piety is empty, no religion absolutely false, no prayer vain," which may be true, if taken in its proper sense, is entirely different from reasoning as if these words meant: all forms of piety are complete, all religions are good, all prayers are effective in relation to the circumstances, the times, and the people who produce them. This would be the apotheosis of religious individualism; but is it not also a complete absurdity? Because it is recognized that there is only one true religion and one perfect revelation, it must also be recognized that many religions have departed on a grand scale from this pattern, not only by failing to achieve it, but also by departing more and more from the inferior version they possessed from the beginning, by refusing to improve it, and by becoming an obstacle to the religious and moral progress of their faithful. The relativity inherent in all human realizations of truth, justice, and piety will not excuse such faults. A religion which ceases to raise man above himself, to tear him free from his passions, his egoism, and the adoration of his own mind, misses its mark and is a religion no more than human: it is false religion, not divine revelation. True religion is religion which has as its law of existence continuous progress in the knowledge of God and the moral education of man. Now, history shows us only one such religion, and, with all due respect to the rationalist who defers disdainfully to all religions without accepting any, and with all due respect to the individualist Protestant who admires in his own person the highest revelation of God, this unique religion was, up to the time of Jesus, the Israelite religion and, since Jesus, has been Catholic Christianity.

* Sabatier, *op. cit.*, 34.

Nevertheless, that all religions have and do acquire from revelation whatever may be true and sanctifying in them, is what the Fathers in early times admitted in their fashion when they showed that the pagan cults and religious teachings of antiquity contained false imitations of biblical revelation and shreds of religious truth borrowed from the same source; this is also what modern apologists mean by the great symbol of primitive revelation handed down from Adam through the ages, from which arose all the polytheist religions of antiquity by a long process of deformation; the same is also indirectly acknowledged by theologians when they affirm that ever since the beginning God has exerted a supernatural influence in all souls, providing each with the help sufficient for it to gain salvation, and that man's damnation can never be attributed other than to his own bad will. These theoretical conceptions assume that every system of worship contains some sound element suited to serve as vehicle for the light of grace and its inspiration, and that that element has indeed never ceased to function as the vehicle of that light and inspiration. It would be no exaggeration to say that this element is prayer in all the different forms in which it remains true prayer, that is to say, a movement of infinite trust in the sovereign power upon which man knows himself entirely dependent. Thus understood, the tradition of prayer found to a greater or lesser extent in those religions which have remained true to their name is an affair neither of pure reason, nor of blind instinct, nor of hereditary prejudice, but a permanent witness to the action on souls of the divine. This divine action upon the mass of humanity must be considered as of the same order as the action of revelation in men inspired. The difference between the poor savage whom God illumines in order to enable him to find life in his wretched system of worship, and the prophet who serves as organ of the most perfect revelation of religious truth lies only in the degree of supernatural light and the extent of the object thus illuminated by faith: the quality of the light and the substance of that object remain identical. In other words, there are several economies of revelation and salvation for humanity. But although even the humblest religion may contain in itself something which renders it salutary for souls, this should not lead one to conclude that every religion is a manifestation both adequate and proportionate to man's needs, the true and relatively complete expression of divine revelation. True religion exists where God has manifested himself completely, where salvation is attached not to mere remnants of tradition entirely without guarantee, but to an institution which is, in itself, the realization of salvation which it serves in a regularly and providentially organized fashion, and outside which there is no real salvation because it preserves the true religion, because it is this true religion, the only one whose essential element is light and life, and whose fundamental principle is to advance in light and in life. Other religions strike the observer as organisms which are either petrified or on the road to dissolution. They may contain some strand which is still alive or susceptible of animation by the divine Spirit, but the Spirit's normal field of action is elsewhere; it is elsewhere that it has its true organ, unique and universal, necessary and permanent, the only one which brings religion and revelation to man.

III

Must revelation now be considered as the sudden and violent introduction of fully formed ideas into a human intellect and a human brain? Mr. Sabatier would like to persuade us that this is the doctrine of the Catholic Church, and is ready, if need be, to demonstrate that it must be so because, according to him, this is how revelation was understood by the prophets. The difference between the mythological notion and the theological notion, or what is claimed as such, is assumed to be no greater than that between poetry and prose, and the theological notion is, we are told, still "entirely pagan."* The learned author is prey to a confusion not unusual among Protestant, rationalist historians of Christian dogma, a confusion which consists in taking an ancient and popular symbol, long maintained or even currently preserved in common teaching and everyday language, as the full and definitive expression of the idea represented by the symbol, without regard to the distinction which exists as a seed in the Scriptures and which is expressly recognized by theology, between religious truth, its essential idea, and the sensory representation through which the idea is as it were made incarnate for the purpose of representing the truth.[†]

---

* *Op cit.*, 44.

[†] "Our modern historians of dogma frequently confuse the image bound up with the use of such an expression with the doctrinal idea. It is the images and formulas in use among primitive authors which are claimed to be in opposition to the doctrines of later authors and the ecumenical councils. This is because, for these writers, all religious knowledge is reduced to a subjective element of the sensory order, in other words, a pure symbol. Whereas Catholic theory acknowledges a spiritual concept bound up with the sensory symbol, the representation, and the means of knowledge, these agnostics challenge the validity of any spiritual knowledge accessory to the symbolic image." De la Barre, *op. cit.*, 202.

It must be recognized that we ourselves still happily discuss revelation in the simple terms suggested by biblical narratives. We think that the first man, born adult by a special act of God's almighty power, could not have been created as an empty soul, but must have enjoyed the perfect exercise of his faculties, and have had an intellect furnished with all the notions we now acquire from teaching and experience. God is supposed to have equipped Adam with a complete store of particular knowledge and words, upon which, after many vicissitudes and transformations, we still live. Such is the conception underlying traditionalism's philosophic theory which it has never been difficult to associate with the theological symbol of primitive revelation. It is not our present task to speculate on the mystery of creation, nor to provide a commentary on the Genesis narratives in the light of dogma. Let us simply say that the profound meaning of these narratives is already exhausted as soon as we conclude that man, with all he is, all he knows, and all he is worth, comes from God and exists for him. Let us refrain, after that, from wanting to teach God how he made man, for of that we know nothing; or by what means he first made himself known to him, because we do not know; or what particular form was taken by primitive revelation, for it is beyond our grasp. Ancient peoples gave the gods responsibility for the institution of all the arts as well as the systems of worship. The traditionalism which would trace the ideas, language, and religion of humanity back to a unique revelation is no more than a systematized expression of those old mythological beliefs. And our apologetic—for these days it is apologetic rather than theological speculation that is interested in these questions—has inadvertently remained somewhat traditionalist. When it wants to determine what it calls the literal, historical, and traditional sense of the first chapters of Genesis, it sums them up in these terms: God conversed with Adam and during these conversations taught him what he needed to know as father and head of humanity. If one is reluctant to make a schoolteacher of the Eternal, as Saint Gregory of Nyssa so aptly expresses it, one nonetheless allows or seems to allow, in the mind of the first man, some sort of indescribable infusion of ideas and the creation of images, and even words, independent of all external stimulation or sensory impression, without any effort of the intellect and without movement of thought. From time to time does not one defend as the most natural proposition in the world the idea that Adam, when he emerged from the Creator's hands, fell into a trance in which he contemplated the tableau of creation now to be found on the first page of the Bible? One does not stop to ask how man could possibly have been in a psychological state whose preconditions he had not fulfilled; how he could have had ideas which had not been formed in him; how he might have seen anything but shadows in a lesson for which no sensory perception had prepared him. Certain as it is that Mr. Sabatier is wrong to attribute no objective value to what he calls the mythological notion and the theological notion of revelation, it seems equally obvious that one would be entertaining much too mechanical an idea of revelation itself if one were to reduce it to the communication of the right formulas inserted by violent operation into a freshly constructed brain. Let us hasten to add that the latter way of understanding revelation is not truly that of Catholic theology; of this one can be assured, by consulting for example, Saint Thomas Aquinas.* The popular form of the biblical narratives maintains in the common teaching conceptions which scholarly theology has always been careful to explain. Thus one finds in the Scriptures that the patriarchs, Moses, and the prophets were taught by God, either by verbal instruction taking external form in supernatural apparitions or by revelatory dreams and extraordinary visions. It must certainly be said that accounts of apparitions which are not symbolic come into the category of visions, and that a vision is in itself a phenomenon of a physiological and psychological order, neither a peculiarly religious phenomenon nor essentially supernatural. Visions could and did serve as vehicles and adjuncts of revelation in the same way as other phenomena of the same order, such as dreams, have done from time to time. But no one would dare to contend that with regard to the Gospel, the normal means of revelation was the imaginative vision or that the direct illumination of human thought, recollected in God, had no part in it. It seems to be established beyond argument that in antiquity the intensity of sensations, the absence of reflection, a sort of inability to distinguish the imaginary from the real or an impression from its cause or object, gave the imagination an extended influence on human development and, in consequence, also a strong role in the development of religion, even revealed religion. This is not a reason for seeing the vision itself as the revelation, nor for supposing the whole imaginative apparatus of visions and dreams to be a purely supernatural creation, or the content not furnished by the previous experiences of the visionary and the natural conditions of his existence.† It is enough to glance at the visions reported in the Bible to see that the content is of a quite everyday nature, always consisting of objects which the

---

* [Thomas Aquinas,] *Summa Theologiae*, II^a IIae q. 171–74.

† "…the prophesied reality is a matter of indifference to prophecy. This aspect of the prophet's task is not altered by the divine operation. The divine power makes away with anything repugnant to prophecy." Saint Thomas Aquinas, *Summa Theologiae*, II^a IIae, q. 172, a. 3, ad. 1. [Latin original. English translation, Saint Thomas Aquinas, *Summa Theologiae* vol. 45 (2a 2ae 171–78) (New York: McGraw-Hill, n.d.), 37, 39.]

prophet has before him or in his memory every day, and that there is nothing really new except the association of ideas which clings to the imaginary symbol; for the ideas themselves, the simple notions which are as it were the substance of revelation, each taken separately, are not new either, and the originality of the doctrine, if one may so express it, lies essentially in the discernment with which they are combined, and which, in uniting them transforms and enlarges them; it is in this discernment, in the light which brings it to birth and in that which spills out from it, that the revelation, properly speaking, is to be found.* There is nothing to indicate, nor has the Church ever taught, that in those who are the inspired organs of revelation, the movement of thought takes a totally irregular course, or happens under physiological and psychological conditions essentially different from those under which it ordinarily occurs and which are not to be encountered anywhere else. Prophetic dreams and visions are found in all religions, and it goes without saying that they are not in all cases the medium of supernatural revelation. The dignity of revealed religion does not demand that revelation should be assumed to be divine madness or the fruit of an artificial mechanism the very notion of which is inconceivable to philosophy. Revelation is divine instruction fitted to the intellectual condition of the men to whom it was initially addressed, and which it would have been pointless to present to them had they not been able to understand it.

Neither humanity's historical tradition, a tradition which starts thousands of years after man appears in the world, nor science, nor faith apprises us of the real, concrete circumstances in which our first ancestors lived, nor of the first manifestations of reason, morality, and religion on earth. We do at least know from the whole history of human development and from the actual character of this development that nothing is made out of nothing, either in the order of intellectual progress and of civilization or in the order of religious and moral progress, and that, even in the

---

* "...so too different dispositions of images bring out different intellectual species in the mind. However, judgment in the human mind is proportionate to the efficacity of intellectual light.... (Ibid., q. 173, a. 1); Of these two aspects of knowledge, the first looms the larger in prophecy: because judgment is the full fruit of cognition"; ibid., a.2 [Latin original. English translation, *Summa Theologiae* vol. 45, p.57]. The direct infusion of *species intelligibiles*, which Saint Thomas defends in the same article, relies on two examples also to be approached with caution, these being Solomon and the apostles: the wisdom of Solomon was not infused knowledge, and it was through the gift of the Holy Spirit that the apostles came to understand what Jesus had already taught them. Moreover, the word "infusion" should not lead us to suppose that Saint Thomas excluded the formation of *species* in and through the intellect. He intends primarily to affirm God's supernatural agency within this formation, and does not discuss the fact that these *species* are never unrelated to the condition of the spirit in which they are produced and what might be called the natural equipment of the intelligence illuminated by revelation.

order of supernatural religion, it is nature which provides the subject and the material, for the subject is man, and the material a fruit of human activity. All scientific doctrine is born of previous notions, and progress results from new combinations of old ideas perceived by the scientific genius which throws a more satisfactory light on how things are connected together. Even seminal truths of the religious order, which constitute the substance of revelation, were formed by the conjunction of ideas or images which existed previously to these truths in the minds of those who first conceived them: what marked at a certain moment the beginning of revelation was the initial perception of the relationship which must exist between man, conscious of himself, and God present behind the world of phenomena; the development of revealed religion, considered in its intellectual aspect, took place through the perception of new relations, which were at base none other than a more precise determination, on a particular point, of the essential relation caught sight of from the beginning. Unlike perceptions of a purely rational and scientific order, the perception of religious truths is not the fruit of reason alone; it is a work of the intellect, carried out, so to say, at the instigation of the heart, of religious and moral sentiment. This whole work, one which has an increasingly perfect outcome in the Israelite religion and subsequently in the Christian religion, and whose marvelous history we are starting to study scientifically, is not really a work done by man on God; it is first and foremost the work of God in man or of man with God. For it is impossible to understand this perpetual attempt to attain perfection in the order of religious knowledge and moral life, an attempt ever contested yet ever crowned with success, without implying the action of God himself both in the attempt and in the success. It is man who seeks, but God who incites him; it is man who sees, but God who enlightens him. Revelation is expressed in man; but it is God's creation in him, with him, and through him. Like its object, the efficient cause of revelation is supernatural because this cause and this object are God himself; but God acts *in* man, and he is known *by* man.

Also, theology does not tell us that revelation is divine in its intellectual and verbal expression. The Scholastic definition of truth, "the perfect correspondence of the intellect with the thing," already the subject of interpretation when applied to the knowledge of natural things, stands in need of even broader commentary when it is applied to things of the divine order. The human intellect, under its immediate conditions of life, perceives an image of natural things, and, through the mediation of this initial image, it forms a representation of supernatural and divine things, rather than seizing them directly or seeing God face-to-face. Divinity in itself is for us the inaccessible and the indefinable. Revelation is not and cannot be other than the divine humanized, one might almost say humanly personified, and striking advances in revelation in some way bear the individual mark of those who were its providential instruments. A relationship of a supernatural order is profoundly experienced in a soul which realizes it in itself, and this relationship is expressed in a symbol sufficiently lively to provoke in other souls a perception of the same relationship in a similar form, which participates in the divine life with which the first symbol was imbued. It is thus that the Holy God of Moses and Isaiah, the type of the servant of Yahweh, the mystery of divine justice in Job, the doctrine of election and faith found in Saint Paul, and even the religion of the Father in the Gospel, which are religious symbols of perpetual and universal value, are, in origin, eminently personal or rather personally experienced conceptions of divine truths humanly realized. One might accumulate a host of different metaphors on this subject without making it any clearer. For, in the religious order, our most consistent ideas are never more than metaphors and symbols, a sort of algebraic notation representing ineffable qualities. If we consider the subject who is the repository and organ of revelation, we may say that it is an education of human souls, supernaturally guided by God ever since the beginning; if we look at its external result, at the symbols which define it, it is a human conception, having been received by human intelligence to whose proportions it is bound to correspond; if we look at its superior principle, at its real object and at the spirit which wholly penetrates it, which was alive in its organs and still lives in its symbols, it is divine; and thence comes its suprarational self-evidence accessible to whoever is animated by the spirit which produced it. All theologians admit that revelation, in its intellectual form and verbal expression, consists of ideas brought to birth in humanity, ideas such as human intelligence was able to perceive, such as could not have existed anywhere else than in a human intellect, such as human language is capable of translating. In relation to the reality they represent they are imperfect symbols, which their very imperfection would render unsatisfactory for intelligence higher than ours, and which, even for us, because they are human in form, are susceptible of explication, which is to say of modification and relative improvement.* Revelation is not immutable in a sense which would mean that these symbols, once given, were immune to all transformation, but because it remains,

---

* "Catholic dogmas are, after all, but symbols of a Divine fact, which, far from being compassed by those very propositions, would not be exhausted, nor fathomed a thousand." John Henry Newman, *Oxford University Sermons* [London: Longmans, Green, 1892], 332.

for faith, always substantially identical with itself, and because the changes which occur in its external determination and in its doctrinal formulas are secondary relative to the permanent unity of its spirit and real continuity of its development.

IV

The work of revelation which we observe from outside, reflecting on it and following it as a development of intellectual knowledge, is not, we have already said, a work of the reason operating alone and in itself on the natural objects of perception, nor a work of man constructing the framework of his religious life and moral progress out of his own resources and his own strength. It should not be regarded as a series of deductions, mutually interconnected, which the more gifted or more attentive of minds may successively have extracted from principles partially seen from the beginning. The revelation of God is a revelation, that is to say, it does not consist of discoveries made by man himself in the order of religious knowledge, but in real communications of divine truths, only in their presentation adapted to the general conditions of nature and human intelligence, as well as to the special and personal conditions of those who first perceived and formulated them. Whatever may have been the external circumstances and sensory forms of these communications, for us they come down to a certain number of essential intuitions, assertions of faith and associations of ideas which were not produced by a voluntary effort of the mind, and whose certitude is not guaranteed by the testimony of reason. These assertions of faith, crowned by the revelation of the Gospel, are seen in the end to come together in harmony, not as if they were logically connected abstract elements of a rational system, but in the delineation of the elements of a life both unique and superior, the divine life which has grown in humanity through the development of true religion, and which persists in Christian souls. The harmony of revelation is a harmony of things rather than a harmony of ideas, and reason has entirely failed to locate this harmony of divine things; all it can do is to acknowledge it when shown it by the light of faith. Each of the essential assertions which constitute objective revelation started off by being a subjective revelation, an assertion by God himself speaking to the conscience of a human being, and this assertion was a manifestation of God, which in this way carried its own absolute certainty for the person favored with it. The historical and psychological forms of divine revelation have been many and various: *multifariam multisque modis locutus est Deus* [God spoke at sundry times and in divers manners], says the Epistle to the Hebrews. We are not required to examine them in detail. It is enough to indicate what has been the basis of all revelation: the perception of a divine truth which came to light in a human intellect by divine operation, with the authority of a divine witness. The real, perceptible pledges of this witness have varied like its forms and according to them. The forms and pledges of the witness have been proportionate to the state of the mind and soul of those to whom the witness was addressed. The witness has been given in terms simple enough to be understood; it has been guaranteed sufficiently to be admitted without hesitation.

Revelation's self-evidence is a consequence, one could say, of the fact that revelation is not a revealed theory but a manifestation of life, a revealed life, a principle of supernatural regeneration. The fundamental truths of religion have not been communicated in the form of speculative teaching, but as divine facts in some fashion experienced by those who perceived them, at the actual time when their minds conceived of their intellectual representation, who were unable to doubt them because these truths became soul of their soul, life of their life. The external signs and all the reasoned proofs of revelation always were and still remain subordinate to this intimate witness which illuminates and unites them in the unshakable certitude of faith.

It is perfectly natural for speculative theology to consider revealed religion as traditional teaching: it is not unaware that this teaching is the expression of a profound reality which contains and overflows doctrine. But the science of religions and the history of dogmas too often abstract from reality and come to see nothing more than a succession of ideas and formulas. Now, religion has always been something other than doctrine; it has never been exhausted in a formula. The religion of the first men was not entirely circumscribed in the idea of the Divinity and his relations with man which they invented for themselves; nor was the Israelite religion entirely circumscribed by the idea which Moses and the prophets conceived of the God of Israel who was also God of the world; nor has the Christian religion reached its final climax in the conception of the Kingdom of Heaven; nor has Catholicism poured its whole self into decrees of councils and manuals of theology. Religion is a reality before it is a theory; it is a spirit before it is an idea; it is a life before it is a formula; and the theory sets out only one aspect of the reality, the idea is no more than an imperfect expression of the spirit; the formula an inadequate manifestation of the life. Revealed religion, that is, the supernatural operation of God in humanity, is therefore not entirely contained in the movement of human thought on religious subjects, even though and inasmuch as this movement is instigated and made fertile by God. Revelation formulated in human language has never been an adequate image of living revelation, of the divine mystery perpetually realized in humanity by religion. Revealed religion is a life, an active organism, a fruitful institution before being a doctrine. Doctrine is an element of religion: it falls far short of being the whole of religion; it is, in a sense, only the intellectual expression, religion's own reflecting consciousness of itself in man, with the positive concurrence and assistance of the God who produces it. This consciousness is such that man may acquire it. It is no clearer than the consciousness a man may have of his own nature; and just as the psychological knowledge of humanity does not represent all the resources hidden in human nature, so the supernatural knowledge which religious humanity, instructed by revelation, that is, by the Church, in the most general sense of the word, may have of religion, of the principle of eternal life which subsists in its bosom, of the God who constantly acts and manifests himself in the many realizations of this principle, does not represent the whole of the intimate force and inexhaustible efficacity of the divine gift. In other words, religion expressed in conceptions and doctrines is no more than a part of experienced religion, one of its indispensable manifestations, but not the whole of religion, nor the whole of the supernatural of religion, nor even, at any instant, the total expression of religion. And as lived religion is a fruitful process, always the same in principle and always new in its manifestations, the religion expressed participates in this same character, a substantial identity underlying an incessant development and perfection of the symbols which embody, as far as may be possible and necessary, the vital development of religion. The religion of the first men was therefore no more a learned theory than ours is a taught theology: it was a divine life whose intellectual expression was necessarily related to their state of mind, and which was designed to reach perfection with time, little by little, as religion itself produced the fullness of its fruits in humanity. Is it not true that this real notion of revealed religion is something quite different from Mr. Sabatier's sentimental intellectualism, and that it forestalls the supposedly inevitable conflict between theological dogma and faith? We shall have the opportunity of returning to the latter point at greater length.

The Proofs and the Economy of Revelation

According to Mr. Sabatier, the traditional notion of revealed religion, that is, the idea of a "divine doctrine legitimated by divine signs or miracles," is not only inconsistent in itself, but also fails in its proofs. In a previous article we saw that in the true meaning of Catholic tradition religion is not simply a doctrine, and we may conclude from this, before any further verification, that the symbols through which this ever-living religion is expressed are not in the least static doctrine.* Let us now come to the proof of revealed religion. It must be concluded that Mr. Sabatier has understood these no better than the very notions of religion and revelation. "Because of the passage of time," he tells us, "the uncertainty of the documents and the requirements of modern thought, the miracle, which in former times established the truth of religion, has become much more difficult to demonstrate than the religion itself."† As for prophecies, "it may be said that the messianic prophecies, insofar as they have a historical and grammatical sense, were never fulfilled, and that they do not seem to have been so in the life, teaching, and death of Jesus Christ and the marvelous development of his work, except in a sense in which they were certainly not understood by those who first uttered them."‡ It remains to be seen whether the miracles of which Mr. Sabatier speaks are all the miracles used to establish the authority of revealed religion, and whether the latter uses them to establish its own authority in the way he supposes: that is to say, as it were by absolute argument or mathematical proof. It remains to be seen whether, for prophecies to be what their name suggests and to retain a demonstrative value, it is indispensable that their authors should have

---

* "Therefore, let there be growth...and all possible progress in understanding, knowledge and wisdom whether in single individuals or in the whole body, in each man as well as in the entire Church, according to the stage of their development; but only within proper limits, that is, in the same doctrine, in the same meaning, and in the same purport." Vatican Council I, *Dogmatic Constitution Dei Filius*, chapt. 4 [Latin original. English translation *The Church Teaches* (St. Louis, Mo.: B. Herder, 1964), 34].

† *Op. cit.*, 45.

‡ *Op. cit.*, 98.

had a rigorously historical preknowledge of the object which realized their predictions.

I

We do not want to discuss the notion of the miracle here, for our humble investigations are of an apologetic and historical nature and not directly philosophical or theological. Yet it must be observed that when Mr. Sabatier says that men of long ago considered miracles as "events uniquely brought about, against the natural course of things, by the intervention of a specific divine act of will,"* he has not conveyed precisely the impression given by the Scriptural narratives. In ancient thought, especially that of biblical antiquity, there was no natural course of things, because there was no concept of the laws of nature. The daily rising of the sun or the occurrence of a shower of rain were as much the result of a specific act of will as Joshua's stopping of the sun in its course and the shadow moving backward on Achaz's dial. Therefore, the miracle does not lie in the specific act of will, for this specific act of will is intrinsic to every natural phenomenon, but in a singular or extraordinary act of the divine will. A miracle does not infringe the order of nature as it was conceived by the men of antiquity. On the other hand, when Mr. Sabatier declared that "the theory of an ascending evolution of beings makes miracles unnecessary,"† he resolves the question of the miracle even before he begins to consider it: if he had wanted to say that evolution explained all the facts thought of as miraculous, he should have applied his principle and shown how the miracles in the Gospel were the fruit of evolution.

From the fact that the significance of a miracle is clearly visible only to faith, conclusions may not be drawn against its reality, for the same is true of divine action in all its manifestations. "Since for philosophy no contingent fact is impossible," we are told by a Christian philosopher,‡ "since the idea of fixed general laws of nature and that of nature itself is only an idol; since every phenomenon is a special case and a unique solution, there is nothing more in a miracle, if one thinks it out fully, than in the most ordinary events.

---

* *Op. cit.*, 69.

† *Op. cit.*, 89.

‡ Maurice Blondel, "Les exigences de la pensée contemporaine en matière d'apologétique," 9–10. [English translation in *The Letter on Apologetics & History and Dogma*, trans. Alexander Dru and Illtyd Trethowan (London: Harvill Press, 1964; repr., Grand Rapids, Mich.: Eerdmans, 1994), 135.]

The purpose of these interventions, which provoke reflection into making conclusions of a more general character by breaking through the deadening effects of routine, is to show that the divine is to be found not only in what seems to surpass the familiar powers of man and of nature but everywhere, even where we are tempted to think that man and nature are sufficient. So miracles are truly miraculous only for those who are already prepared to recognize the divine action in the most usual events. And it follows that philosophy, which would offend against its own nature by denying them, is no less incompetent to affirm them, and that they are a witness written in a language other than that of which it is the judge." If we have understood Mr. Blondel aright, he wishes to say that for the philosopher or scholar as such, everything which happens is what could happen: what, under the given factual conditions, had to happen; from which it follows that a miracle is an extraordinary fact the divine significance of which is appreciable only by whoever believes in the action of Providence in everyday occurrences. This doctrine is not exactly new, for, up to a certain point it can claim authority from Saint Augustine.* It seems to us that it might be expressed as follows: just as a miracle, among primitive peoples and seen with the eye of faith, is no more than a divine action somewhat more perceptible than others, so from a rational and scientific point of view, the best observed miracle is nothing but a fact less common than others but which must be included in the same order as the others, because it really is part of that order; properly speaking, a miracle is the course of events in the world and life contemplated by faith which is unique in its capacity to penetrate its mystery; the same events in the world and life, observed to some degree from the outside, through the reason, are the order of nature, the domain of science and of philosophy.

This conception of the miracle is not the one adopted by modern theologians as a whole. Nor is it offered here as a thesis worthy of complete approval, but as a purely philosophical and historical way of looking at a problem whose theological solution is not without obscurities. In considering the laws of nature as something absolute, theologians see no difficulty in explaining certain extraordinary facts by attributing them to diabolical action. For the purpose of distinguishing such diabolical miracles from divine miracles, the notion of natural law becomes an inadequate criterion, and it is according to the moral circumstances of the fact that its character is determined. But the fundamental difficulty lies elsewhere; it lies in the

---

* *De utilitate credendi* [On the Profit of Believing], 16; *De civitate Dei* [The City of God], XXI, 8.

very notion of the law. The accepted idea of a miracle assumes that the laws of nature are in themselves what we are capable of knowing about them. Now, Mr. Sabatier, Mr. Blondel, and many others point out that our conceptions are not the law of existence and that what we designate as laws are certain general ideas which are simply the abstract categories in which we sum up the working of our minds on entirely relative and incomplete experiences. And it is certain indeed that if, because of the constitution of our reason we are unable to conceive of the world as other than governed by the sequence of cause and effect, we shall no more hit on the intimate law of things by our reflection than we hit on the intimate nature of things through our experience. This is why we will leave to the professional theologians the business of discussing theoretical notions of law and miracle. Leaving aside all metaphysical definition, the facts remain facts, and the testimony to himself which God provides in extraordinary facts subsists side by side with that which he provides in ordinary facts. However one may analyze them or interpret them in philosophy, the two testimonies subsist in the reality of nature and history. Although they fail to make complete sense except to faith, they both, one and the other, command attention from the reason, and the reason may not set either one or other of them aside.

One reads in the decrees of the last ecumenical council: "…in order that the submission of our faith might be consonant with reason, God has willed that external proofs of his revelation, namely, divine acts and especially miracles and prophecies, should be added to the interior aids given by the Holy Spirit. Since these proofs so excellently display God's omnipotence and limitless knowledge, they constitute the surest signs of divine revelation, signs that are suitable to everyone's understanding. Therefore not only Moses and the prophets, but also preeminently Christ our Lord, performed many evident miracles and prophecies."* The same council pronounces anathema against "anyone [who] says that miracles are impossible and, hence, that all accounts of them, even though contained in the Sacred Scripture, should be classed with fables and myths; or that miracles can never be recognized with certainty and that the divine origin of the Christian religion cannot be successfully be proved by them." Like all dogmatic definitions, these definitions are protective devices against a particular error, and in order to hear them aright one must look at the error they are contesting. They are visibly aimed against those who a priori deny the actual

---

* Const. *Dei Filius*, III.

reality of the facts which form the historical foundation of religion, or who contest them as divine effects recognizable as such, who will allow the accounts of the two Testaments neither providential significance nor conclusive authority. The council does not wish the miraculous accounts found in the Scriptures to be regarded as myths and lying inventions, or as an erroneous interpretation of real facts, nor that prophecies should be claimed to represent no more than contradictions of tradition. It condemns Strauss and Renan and biblical rationalism in general. In spite of appearances, the teaching of the council is more negative than positive; for although it rejects the explanations of unbelieving rationalism, it does not determine what constitutes the reality of either miracle or prophecy, nor in what manner that reality may serve as a solid proof of religion. Scholastic notions of miracle and prophecy, the well-known arguments of traditional apologetics, are present in the background of the definition without being its object, and without receiving any further explanation. The council has not set out the proof whose existence and value it affirms; it has not translated it into the language of modern science. This work did not lie within either its intention or its role.

The Vatican Council did not provide a scientific definition either of miracles or of prophecies; but it did indicate their essential character; they are divine facts, and it is the divine fact that is proof of religion. A divine fact is one in which God makes himself known to the well-disposed soul. The great divine fact is religion itself in its continued progress, from its humble and distant origins up to Jesus the Savior and, since Jesus, in the Church. This great supernatural fact is like a web of extremely varied divine manifestations, each of which may itself may be considered a divine fact, inexplicable to the reason, and from that very circumstance, to the eye of faith a true revelation of God. The specific acts which one groups together under the terms "miracles" and "prophecies" are no more than the most obvious category of these divine facts, all of which are, at bottom, true miracles. It is the entirety of religious development, as a whole and in its details, in the person of its foremost agents, in their speech and in their actions, which is extraordinary. Each fact separately does not contain the absolute evidence of its divine character, because no such evidence exists, in the matter either of fact or of history. From a rational point of view, one has no more than a moral certitude of the things narrated; as for those of which one is oneself a witness, their physical certainty is limited by the actual conditions of observation, and when it comes to superior causes and to the metaphysical conditions of the fact observed, it is the realm of hypothesis and not that of certitude which is displayed; for an unprejudiced spirit, the supernatural explanation may be the only one to unite all the characteristics of the representation, but this hypothesis is not an absolute necessity, because the reasoning which supports it points to two objects which we are unable to perceive directly, the intimate reality of things and the being of God. A miracle is not evident as such except to faith.

This is why Christianity's demonstration will not perhaps gain overmuch from the distinction now so readily made between miracles of providence and proper miracles. This distinction does not seem to have much bearing on the faith, which has always seen as true miracles what are called miracles of providence, and, reciprocally, as miracles of providence miracles properly speaking. Nor does it have greater implication from the point of view of science, where no other distinction between facts is known than what may follow from their specific nature, from their form, and from the guarantee afforded by their historical attestation. The divine fact, inasmuch as it is divine, is not absolutely evident to the reason before the latter contemplates it in the light of faith. Now the miracle is in the divine fact. The accumulation of extraordinary facts which constitutes the history of religion is, from a rational point of view, an accumulation of probabilities in favor of its divinity and, does one dare to add, in favor of God himself. The susceptibility of faith to reason results from this accumulation which is the rational basis of certitude in the moral order; but the absolute certainty of the divine fact does not and cannot result from its proofs; it is born of a superior light which illuminates the proofs and the facts themselves, and which is the light of faith.

In this series of facts and proofs, miracles keep their place and it is a preeminent one, because they are still the most salient features of the religious phenomenon taken as a whole. For the object is not, as Mr. Sabatier supposes, to discover "whether there are or have ever been phenomena which must be attributed to direct intervention by God and to a specific act of his will, independently of the natural concurrence of secondary causes."* And if the question were so expressed, one cannot see how this would be "clearly something which only critical observation of past and present facts can tell us," considering that, according to Mr. Sabatier himself, "science knows none but secondary causes."† This comes down to saying that science is able to observe the material reality of a fact but that

---

* *Op. cit.*, 65.
† *Op. cit.*, 85.

it is powerless to demonstrate, scientifically or mathematically, its divine character. Now, it is not in the nature of the divine fact to be so demonstrated, and the incapacity of the reason is no more than a recognition of its own limits, which proves nothing against the divinity of the fact. But it is not the "how" of the divine action which is at issue here, it is its reality. The "how" is a mystery, it escapes science, and faith can express it only by imperfect analogies. The reality of the divine action is defined in the actual effect which attracts the attention of the reason and prepares the way for faith. Miracles are facts that are religious or in close relation to religion and inexplicable as natural effects. They are not, as such, explicable by the unaided reason as supernatural effects, the reason being without the criterion of the supernatural among its own principles. They nonetheless subsist for the reason as actual facts, for which divine action furnishes an explanation adequate if not absolutely certain for each particular case. The gospel miracles, for example, are not to be explained by science as natural facts; they nonetheless present themselves even to science as real facts, and, given the conditions under which they happened, as extraordinary facts for which there is no other plausible explanation than that of a supernatural action, of a divine action. This is undoubtedly sufficient for the purpose of retaining for miracles, in their role of religious proof and inasmuch as this proof does not appeal to the intellect alone but to the religious soul, to every well-disposed soul, the character of an "extremely sure testimony to divine revelation." After reducing religion to a vague sentiment, Mr. Sabatier looks on the whole history of religion on earth as not having occurred. But this history remains, and it is a divine history which gives very real witness to true religion, to that which exists now and which is heir to that divine past, to Catholic Christianity.

II

What has just been said about miracles also has its application with respect to prophecies. One could take them one after the other, all those cited in the New Testament, all those which have kept their place in the books of apologetics, from the serpent's curse in Genesis up to the symbolic descriptions of the Apocalypse, without finding more than a few which, for those who wrote them down, clearly bore the precise meaning attributed to them by tradition, or which would obviously be predictions, that is to say, miracles of prescience, in the strict sense of the word.* The liberty which we see taken by the New Testament in its interpretation of the Old, and the use of an exegesis which allowed the discovery in certain passages, taken out of context, of messianic prophecies in the most precise sense, may be explained, from a historical point of view, by habits of mind very remote from our own. From the theological point of view, the differences which one notices between the natural sense of the texts and their prophetic application are to be explained by the theory of the spiritual sense. For an entirely exterior and superficial criticism, the spiritual sense of the prophecies is no more than an accommodation authorized by the New Testament or the witness of tradition, while the sense described as *accommodating* is a new application whose sole recommendation is the personal authority or ingenuity of the person who proposes it. Not only does it seem impossible to establish, by the agreement between ancient predictions and the facts put forward as their fulfillment, any plain and indisputable proof of a prescience which the agents of the revelation could only have received from God; but the apologist is almost obliged to justify a method of argumentation which appears to be founded on artificial correspondences. Mr. Sabatier has already told us that all the messianic prophecies were false, since the Messiah was not what the prophets said, and he compares "prophetic divination" to "ancient mantic practices," at which "everyone laughed" as long ago as "Cicero's time."†

But if the exegesis of the spiritual sense, which is so widely practiced in the New Testament, which the Fathers retained and developed, which was an important factor in dogmatic development and theology in all ages of history, and which has kept its position in Christian teaching up to the present day, may seem arbitrary in its details and procedures, since it is externally based only on analogies of varying consistency and which one would sometimes class as purely verbal, it is nonetheless erected as a whole on an incontestable principle: the intimate and constant harmony of ideas and things in a religious movement which has come to pass little by little under the guidance of Providence. By spreading it over a quantity of texts whose primitive meaning they almost unconsciously modified or enlarged, the old interpreters justified a general argument which still retains all its force, that is, the perceptible continuity of providential action in the growth of

---

* Cf. Abbé de Broglie, *Questions bibliques* [Paris: Victor Lecoffre, 1897], 374–80. [On Albert de Broglie, see François Laplanche, *Dictionnaire du monde religieux dans le France contemporaine*, vol. 9, *Les sciences religieuses* (Paris: Beauchesne, 1996), 108–10].

† *Op. cit.*, 93.

monotheistic religion, and the essential and profound bond which exists between all the phases of its history. Seen from outside, the work of exegesis built up by Christian tradition on the Old Testament and the prophetic parts of the New seems to be attached to the scriptural texts by a thousand contrivances; it is certainly attuned to a particular state of biblical knowledge and a general state of human knowledge which have now been overtaken. But if one enters into the spirit of the Scriptures and their interpreters the effect is entirely different. If the explanation of each passage taken separately does not represent the strictly historical sense of the text, the explanation of all the passages taken together represents what might be called the inexhaustible providential sense of the Old Testament and all the prophecies: the development which the seeds planted in the Scriptures were destined to receive through the manifestation and onward movement of the Gospel, the perpetual consciousness of its own identity that true religion has kept through every time and change. The exegesis of the spiritual sense, like all the workings of religious thought in the two Testaments and in the Church, is a manifestation of the Spirit of truth. It is a narrow and sluggish mind which will refuse to see in the traditional interpretation of the prophecies anything more than an interminable series of contradictions, serious or slight. This exegesis did not claim to be historical and literal in its time, when the sense of history and the conditions imposed on the historical interpretation of texts hardly existed. The Apostles drew on the authority of the Old Testament for their preaching of Christ and the Gospel because, in a very true sense, the Old Testament prepares for, announces, and prefigures the New. This truth could not then be conceived of or demonstrated in an abstract and scholarly form. One went back to the Scriptures themselves, dissected and interpreted according to the custom of Jewish exegesis, in order to establish the correlation between the two Testaments in the spirit which enlivens, as against the letter which kills. The thesis was indeed a solid one, despite the relative imperfections of the form it was obliged to adopt. It remains a very telling argument in favor of Catholic Christianity.

Whatever may have been the particular meaning of this or that text, and in whatever way theology may explain the relation of these texts to their traditional interpretation and interpret the very theory of the spiritual sense, the Scriptures emerge as a vast compilation of religious hopes and aspirations, certain hopes and infinite aspirations. The birth, progress, and partial and successive fulfillment of these hopes and aspirations, which move onward attended by an enlargement and spiritualization in proportion to the defeats inflicted on them by the brutality of events, are an admirable lesson for faith; and the precursors of ideas and religious principles not perfectly realized until later are a proof of providential action in the history of religion which cannot be neglected. The critics may discourse at will on the circumstances which suggested the idea of the servant of God in the second part of Isaiah; the relation of this idea to the very conception of the Gospel remains a fact which transcends all vulgar explanation and to which faith alone holds the key. If it is true that Israel's hopes bear the mark of the times and social circumstances in which they were expressed, it is nonetheless belittling to the messianic prophecies to consider them "entirely Jewish, concerned with the Jewish people, not the Christian Church to which they are applied," and to say that "the Jews, according to their exegesis, may quite well have failed to see in Jesus of Nazareth the Messiah they were waiting for, since they could not have believed in him without renouncing the political and national hopes with which their books had provided them."* The books of the Old Testament were written by Israelites and for Israelites; they nevertheless contain, often but not always associated with the still imperfect images in which the national spirit expresses itself, the announcement of a spiritual and universal reign of God. This announcement was the true gospel preparation, and Jesus had the right to derive his authority from it. The prophetic spirit was already the spirit of the Gospel. Only the framework of the prophecies was national, and most of the Jews wanted to confine themselves to that in the framework of messianic hope: there is no occasion to praise their exegesis, which was no more faithful to the historical sense of the prophecies than that of the New Testament and which completely failed to recognize its spirit, that is to say, its true religious and providential meaning.†

Nothing is more homogeneous at bottom, more logical in its perpetual rejuvenation, than the messianic hope from the time of the most ancient prophets down to the preaching of the kingdom of heaven and the Johannine Apocalypse. The cold reasoning of the scholar sees in it no more than a succession of illusions more or less fanciful and regularly disappointed; and yet it is only the form of the hope, its imaginative color, which is relative and fragile; the hope itself, the intuition of the triumph which is being stored up and prepared by eternal justice and mercy, is a fact unique of its kind, inexplicable in itself, truly supernatural; the

* *Op. cit.*, 92.

† "The future almost always turns out differently from our expectations; and even the things which God has revealed about it take place in ways which we should never have predicted." [Jacques-Benigne] Bossuet, *L'Apocalypse*, xv.

progressive refinement of this hope and its realization, which has begun and is ever carried forward in the Gospel and in the Church, are the great prophecy, that which encompasses and validates all the others, that which has remained unshaken by criticism, which still speaks to a religious spirit, which has always been recognized by well-disposed souls. Criticism may analyze the apparent origins, the historical development, and the external transformations of the messianic ideal; it will not discover in history the real cause, the satisfactory explanation of the phenomenon it would have liked to study. The argument of the prophecies, properly understood, remains therefore, with that of miracles one of those probabilities or rather one of those categories of probabilities which witness to revealed religion, and which, for faith, turn into purposes which are sure, even in their own way evident, when they appear in their true light, the light of God who has spoken through the prophets and in the Gospel.

Whatever learned doctors may think of Christian subjectivity, it is by that path that the inspiration of the prophets is shown to be something supernatural in principle, with a supernatural object and a vital and providential correspondence to the Gospel and Christianity. To say that "religious inspiration is psychologically no different from poetic inspiration," that it "certainly provides the same mystery, but carries no greater implication of miracle,"* is to show how much store is being set on suppressing the objective value of revelation and making religion into a purely human phenomenon: the author is quite ready to confuse illuminism with religious inspiration, and to find religion everywhere so as not to have to acknowledge it where it is. Prophecy is a divine fact; and poetic inspiration, as such, however mysterious its origin, is not a divine fact. Actions are specified by their object and not by the analogy of their psychological forms. Mr. Sabatier, for whom the cult of the beautiful is a religion, has no difficulty in putting poetic inspiration on the same footing as religious inspiration. But it is also easy to see how the one differs from the other if it has not been decided in advance that religion should be regarded as just any movement of the soul. It is of no use, after having denied the objective value of prophetic inspiration, to write that "it is piety raised to the second power";† for this merely raises "to the second power" the negation initially expressed.‡

---

* *Op. cit.*, 99–100.

† *Op. cit.*, 100.

‡ It is not at all part of our purpose to draw attention to certain inaccuracies which are to be found in Mr. Sabatier's book in the matter of biblical, ecclesiastical, or theological history. However, it would

III

In this way the proofs of Christianity stand up to individualistic criticism. It is necessary only to understand them properly in order to reap their profit and present them to others in a useful manner. The proof of miracles is allied to the demonstration of all the good things which religion has obtained and obtains, and which only it can obtain for humanity, in Christianity and in the Church. The proof of the prophecies forms part of the demonstration of the harmonious and constant relations of religious development considered over its entire extent, throughout the ages of its existence. The apologetic of the last centuries has seen the truth of religion as above all a thesis to be defended by well-reasoned arguments, just as its adversaries saw in it a thesis to be upset by the same procedure. Contemporary positivism demands that it should be presented as a fact to be observed. In order to be convinced of the unique and extraordinary character of Catholic Christianity it would have the divinity of Catholicism appear before it, "not by virtue of a preconceived idea, but of a truly objective, positive or positivist certainty."* For this let us not take it too much to task, for religion is a fact before it is a theory; let us only be sure we know what experience is at issue and what procedures must be followed in order to take it to its proper conclusion.

One must first of all distinguish the orders of reason and of pure science, of nature and of physical experience, from the religious and moral order, the order of grace and supernatural experience. It is because it demanded absolute rational certainty from religious truths that rationalist science rejected them. If the learned doctors of Christian individualism give up all certainty of belief and no longer see anything more solid in religion than the sentiment of faith, it is because they have similarly confused the conditions of religious and moral certainty with those of scientific certainty and, the latter conditions not being fulfilled in the faith, have not paid any attention to the former, seeing nothing more certain in religion than the existence of the religious faculty. Shall we add that it is because they have failed to establish the precise distinction which exists, with respect to the foundations of certitude and the means of acquiring

---

seem useful to mention the one on page 98 where Saint Thomas Aquinas is credited with a theory of verbal inspiration which has been held by several Protestant theologians but which one will look for in vain in the writings of the Angelic Doctor, beginning with the article of the *Summa* to which Mr. Sabatier refers his reader.

* F. Brunetière, *Revue des Deux Mondes*, t. CL (1898): 719.

it, between truths of a purely scientific and rational order and truths of a religious and moral order, that most of our apologists seem to want to endow Christian proofs with the self-evidence and unchangeableness of a theorem of geometry? Yet the Christian and Catholic act of faith has never been found at the end of a syllogism. No one has ever used mathematical certainty to demonstrate religion. One believes in it because one sees in it the marks of the divine, and this recognition is effected much less by the reason than by reflective or even unconscious observation of what religion is in its living reality, through the interior recollection which consolidates the gains of this observation, and through the moral effort which renews it in a certain way in the believing subject.

Apologetics constructed for the demonstration or defense of religion serve rather to justify and protect the faith in those who possess it than to furnish an irrefutable proof of its truth to those who do not believe. They necessarily follow the line of the objections raised by people outside. Thus the apostles used the prophecies to prove to the Jews that Jesus of Nazareth was the Messiah promised to Israel: Was it because of these texts that they themselves had first believed in him, and was there a single Jew who was won over by this argument without the gospel fact having been presented to him and having revealed to him the spirit of the Scriptures? The apologists of the second century proved the truth of the Gospel to the pagans by showing Christianity as the most perfect of philosophies: Did they see in it nothing else, and did many pagans convert to the new religion as the acme of learned doctrines? Today, the advocates of Catholicism multiply arguments in its favor, and neither system nor institution has ever been defended by so many reasons taken from every quarter: the reason is that the objections come from all quarters, and one is forced to reply to them. But the most far-seeing spirit, after studying the thickest tomes of apologetics, can still be very undecided and perplexed if he has only taken counsel with his faculty for rational argument and if he has limited his inquiry to a criticism of proofs, given that each particular proof leads only to a conclusion which is probable and which does not absolutely exclude the possibility of the opposite, and that the decisive effectiveness of the proofs does not depend entirely on their accumulation, which still presents the reason with no more than a high degree of probability, but on a personal experience of them and on the vital relation established between the inquiring soul and the truth it is offered.

Every conversion, the conscious faith of every Christian, is a separate work, whose genesis and motives are nowhere consigned to writing before it is completed; the motives themselves are not entirely perceived and even less susceptible to full expression by the person under their influence; they would be insufficient, such as they are, to produce conversion in a different person, on the impossible hypothesis that the first subject were able to analyze them in depth and express them fully and clearly; and still the second subject would have to appropriate them for his own use by means of a personal effort which would show him the truth better than any argument. This comes down to saying that the living experience of religion is always more real and more true than its outward proofs; that the best reasons one has for believing are not necessarily to be found in books; that rational probabilities pass beyond doubt when faith illuminates them and discloses their profound unity to the religious soul; that the proofs of religion do not bear faith within them, but simply prepare the way for it, and that, in the believing soul, it is instead faith that bears the proofs in the sense that it endows them with a supernatural self-evidence which as rational arguments of a relative nature they do not possess. Apologetic replies to certain difficulties which are more or less keenly felt at a particular moment, to a general though not permanent state of people's minds; it does not create each person's faith, but it assists in the process; and in order to assist in this way it changes to suit the times, social circumstances, and people, according to the evolution and progress of human knowledge.

The adversaries of religion claim to demonstrate by science and reason the absolute foolishness of religion, and the apologists, from their side, attempt to demonstrate its absolute truth by rational and scientific argument. Unbelievers must first of all be reminded that reason and science are quite incapable in the field of religion, which is not of their order, that they are not competent, on their own, either to produce or to upset the absolute certainty of religious and moral truths. Reason has its part, and it is a necessary part, in the acquisition of this certitude, but it is not sufficient to create it, because the object in question is not within its province. It will build up the probabilities to a point at which it would be imprudent if not foolish not to heed them; it will be able to make the necessity of commitment seem *absolutely reasonable* but not *rationally evident*, which would under any other conditions be devastating and valueless. Total clarity in the order of religious and moral truths is obtained by the concurrence of all the higher faculties of man and not by the mere application of the intellect to the proofs of faith. This is why the best rational demonstration never comprises more than a part of the actual demonstration which occurs in souls, the only one which can be truly conclusive. The profound and universal reason for faith is simply religion's conformity to the need and aspirations of man. Now, this correspondence of the supernatural to our nature, this accommodation of God to our poverty is as much morally sensed as intellectually seen; and it is not an abstract relation discerned by the believer through the use of his mind; it is a reality which is fulfilled in him and by him, by God with him.* Discursive reason is not the indispensable form of this vital and efficacious reason. It is its incomplete expression in cultivated spirits. But faith, in order to be a superior act of reason, does not need to be propped up by a set of logical deductions.

True religion is made to be known, tried, lived, and this personal experience has always been its true demonstration, varying in its logical expression according to the times and even to the people, certain for all those who believe, that is to say, those who, having a close enough view of religion to know it well in itself and in relation to themselves, have the courage to subscribe to it of their own free will. The will intervenes in the act of faith because revealed religion is not a theory to be embraced solely on account of rational conviction. The most learned demonstration makes no difference to these essential conditions of faith. This is what Cardinal Newman wrote: "I say, that I believed in a God on a ground of probability; that I believed in Christianity on a probability; that I believed in Catholicism on a probability; and that these three grounds of probability, distinct from each other of course in subject matter, were still all of them one and the same in nature of proof, as being probabilities—probabilities of a special kind, a cumulative, a transcendent probability but still probability; inasmuch as He who made us has so willed, that in mathematics indeed we should arrive at certitude by rigid demonstration, but in religious inquiry we should arrive at certitude by accumulated probabilities;— He has willed, I say, that we should so act, and, as willing it, He cooperates with us in our acting; and thereby enables us to do that which He wills us to do, and carries us on, if our will does but co-operate with His, to a certitude which rises higher than the logical force of our conclusions."† In other words, the demonstration is completed in the actual reality of faith, in its substantial truth, whence flashes out on the mass of probabilities the ray which lights them, the life which animates them and the unshakable certitude which gathers them together. Faith, we repeat once more, is

---

* All our readers will know how the role of the will in the acquisition of religious and moral truths has been illuminated by Mr. Ollé-Laprune, in particular in his book *Certitude morale*.

† John Henry Newman, *Apologia Pro Vita Sua* [London: Longmans, Green, 1865], 199–200.

nothing if not deeply reasonable, even though it is not a matter of rational speculation; but its superior reason does not reveal itself in its entirety except to those who sincerely want to know it and who are not afraid of the truth. There is nothing to prevent the ignorant succeeding in this in their fashion just as much as the learned, without so much inquiry and discussion.

In being thus understood, the certainty of revelation is not diminished; it is identified with its true character, which is to be a certainty of faith and not a scientific certainty. According to Catholic dogma, faith, even in its beginnings, is a gift from God, not a fruit of human understanding and human activity. What does this mean unless that the proofs of religion are not of such a nature as necessarily to impel man's conviction, judging from the principles of reason alone; that faith is born in the soul in which a divine sense has been aroused which allows it to savor the personal force of the proofs, the supernatural efficacity of the religion proclaimed in the proofs, and in some fashion to find itself, with its aspirations and moral needs, in the religion which satisfies in overstimulating them, and which overstimulates them in order to fill them to overflowing. This divine sense of faith is in no way to be gained by the exercise of argument and criticism; it occurs in the well-disposed soul when the proposed revelation in one way or another comes into contact with the intellect. It is certainly true that faith is a grace, and, at the same time, that we believe because we want to believe. Faith would not need to be a supernatural gift, and it could not be a free act of man if the assent of the mind to the revealed truths were due solely to the rational evidence of the proofs of revelation. A work of pure reason does not call for supernatural aid, and it excludes any use of freedom in respect of the conclusion; for it makes choice impossible. The conclusion is what it is; anyone who will take the trouble to look will find it and will be unable to dissent from it. In the order of religious and moral belief, the conclusion, however legitimate and obligatory it may be, is, in a certain way, what one makes it, and its object will be in some way determined by the act which produces it; as this object is supernatural by nature, in the real, historic economy of salvation, one imagines some enlightenment and vigor of grace as indispensable to seeing it properly and embracing it, and that one is allowed the freedom not to raise oneself as far as God invites one to ascend, not to verify the proposal of faith and consequently not to realize it in oneself. The obscurity of the mysteries and moral obligations which result from the revelation would make the assent of the intellect no less necessary if the preliminary argumentation were absolutely evident.

But religion is not a theorem to be demonstrated like a + b; it is a divine fact which one is free to contemplate or not to contemplate, which is not plain to those who do not want to see it; it is a superior life which one may assimilate just as one may also reject, an economy of salvation into which one may enter, and outside which one may, to one's perdition, remain. It does not follow that faith logically comes before the use of reason and that learned apologetics are of no use, but that reason and apologetics, although they prepare for and set the conditions of faith, would be incapable of creating it. Reason demonstrates the rationality of faith; but the moral certainty it gives to it is not the absolute certitude of faith, a certitude which results from faith itself and which is an action of the soul as a whole, helped by God to recognize him in his revelation.* The rational demonstration and apologetics of religion nonetheless retain their relative necessity. The thesis they defend is always better than the logical form in which they clothe it. It may even happen that the structure of the argumentation is defective and yet its effectiveness is not entirely compromised thereby, because although one does not always demonstrate religion as rigorously as one thinks, one teaches it nonetheless, and religion supplies its own proof to every well-disposed soul who knows it well enough. The duty of theologians and apologists is nevertheless to facilitate as much as possible this understanding of revealed religion by adapting their demonstrations to the intellectual culture and the state of knowledge, chiefly religious knowledge.

This is why it is desirable, in fact, that our apologetics should be transformed more and more into a real, historic demonstration which would bring out the necessity of faith and the impossibility of finding the guarantees of a solid, authoritative, beneficent faith outside Catholic Christianity. In order to remove all occasion for facile and dangerous misunderstandings, all pretext for specious objections masquerading as knowledge and criticism, it is essential to have a good knowledge and give a good explanation of what has been the development of religion through the ages and to reconstitute its sequel, not by a priori argumentation or poetic blunderings nor even by means of the grandiose metaphors of antique symbolism or the abstract reflections of ancient philosophy, but by the facts, the humble facts, which, fragile and fugitive as they may be, now turn out to

---

* "However, even though the assent of faith is by no means a blind impulse, still, no one can 'assent to gospel preaching' as he must in order to be saved 'without the enlightenment and inspiration of the Holy Spirit,' who gives all men their joy in assenting to and believing the truth." *Dei Filius*, III [Latin original. English translation *The Church Teaches*, 29].

be more resistant than syllogisms to all attack. The message and deeds of the prophets are facts; the parables of Jesus are facts, his miracles, his life, his death, his resurrection are facts; the writings of the Fathers and lives of the saints are facts; the Church and its history, its influence in the past and its action in the present are facts; the religious life of humanity throughout the ages, that of Christian and Catholic humanity, is a fact. A proper analysis of this grand fact would be a positive demonstration of Catholic Christianity. Faith consists in a sense in seeing it properly. Its analysis uncovers the traces of God, more and more perceptible as one approaches the Savior and, having encountered him, follows after him who lives and reigns over all. Faith collects up these traces and pieces them together, remaking once again the synthesis of God, of Jesus Christ, and of the Church, and perceiving its harmonious unity all the more clearly the better it has discerned the stages of its astonishing evolution. This demonstration would be new only in form and not in idea; it would not be an abandonment or denial of the traditional method, but a simple transposition or interpretation of the apologetic material, a positive organization of fundamental theology. The defense of Catholicism does not have to be redone as if it were necessary to construct a different theory of faith and its preliminaries. The defenders of Catholic Christianity have only to acquire a more real knowledge of what it is and what it has been, of its present which is the life of religion on earth and of its past which is the history of religion in the world, in order to define it better and to make it better known to men, as it has been, as it is, as it should and wants to be; as true religion this is all the apologetics it needs.

IV

The certitude of faith, founded on real grounds and profoundly experienced by the religious soul, has a specific object. The indefinite is not matter for certitude. The certitude of faith will necessarily apply to God and to his revelation, to God revealing himself and revealed, to a positive and concrete notion of God and of religion, of the effective relation of man to God, and precisely not to the metaphysical relation of the contingent being to the principle of all things. The object of religious certitude is governed, in a certain fashion, by the actual nature of religion and the inevitable conditions of the revelation of God to humanity. This object will consist of truths immutable at their root but not at all fixed in respect of the forms in which they may successively be clothed in the thought and language of men. In order to be certain, revelation never ceases to be progressive, and it may be said that the knowledge of God would come to an end on earth the moment one claimed to have captured it in its entirety in absolute and invariable formulations, because that would be to identify eternal truth with a created symbol, to invent a spiritual idol as cold and dead as idols of stone or wood. Revelation is born alive and remains so in humanity. It would not continue to exist in this world without its organs and means of conservation, which are not to be confused with it, but from which it cannot be separated; it animates and supports them out of its divine spirit, out of its infinite life; it appropriates them and adapts them to its eternal purposes.

Religion is a thing in common, essentially *humanitarian*: one cannot conceive of revelation existing only for isolated individuals, manifesting itself only in them, through them, and for them. Religion has its seat in individuals, like knowledge and virtue; but like them it is a common good, not a personal possession; perfect religion is one of the essential forms, the only universal and permanent form of human society, not a privilege of this or that private person. The true is for all; duty is incumbent upon everybody. God too exists for all and is incumbent upon all. If therefore religion has been established and is maintained in humanity in the form of revelation, if it is the authentic revelation of God, it will exist for all, it will be bound to address all, and thus addressing all men, in all ages, in some sense to accommodate itself to them all. The necessity of religious symbols and of an institution to watch over and interpret these symbols becomes perfectly apparent when religion is looked at in its historical reality of living and enduring revelation. Revelation must have its intellectual and intelligible expression; and there must be authorized interpreters of this expression, because religious formulas will not suffice to transmit religion any more than scientific formulas suffice to transmit science. Science and religion do not travel directly from man to book and from book to man; but from man to man with the aid of the book. The benefit of an acquired revelation will be guaranteed to the human race by the persistence of a living and true teaching, which is to say by an infallible Church, or it will have been for nothing. Revealed religion, since it is not a simple doctrine, but a gift of supernatural life, will be perpetuated wherever it has not ceased to be alive, where it is organized into a teaching and sanctifying institution, setting before all men and communicating to them "the eternal life that was in the Father and that has been manifested to us."*

* 1 Jn. 1.2.

As soon as one ceases to see the formulations of human language as an adequate and perfect expression of religious truth, and religion as the simple acceptance of a doctrinal creed, such an institution becomes indispensable, the formulation not being capable of communicating alone and indefinitely what it was in the beginning incapable of encompassing, and religious truth not being alive unless it is in process of perpetual adaptation in order to fit itself to variable states of intelligence, and incessantly displaying the inexhaustible treasure of the ever-new life which constitutes true religion. Religion and revelation are inconceivable in their relatively perfect state without this permanent institution which will make use of the formulations while continuously perfecting them, which will be the ever-living revelation rendered actually present, which will be the continuation of religion in history and its organ in the world; whereas the idea of a religion wholly comprised in its formulations, as orthodox Protestantism would have it, is a principle of blindness and fanaticism insofar as it is realized, and the idea of revelation without authorized teaching, which belongs to Christian individualism, can be no more than a flight of fancy.

The notion of religion and of revelation, far from excluding the idea of a Church, and an infallible Church, necessarily supposes it. "A social and universal fact as much and more than an individual one, it is in the social life of the species, in organized religious societies, in institutions, the common system of worship, liturgy, rules of faith and of discipline, that religion objectively realizes its fundamental principle, manifests its interior soul and develops all its power. In the same way a religious life which remains hidden in the individual conscience, which is not communicated and which creates no spiritual solidarity, no brotherhood of soul, is as if it did not exist; it is a simply a sentimental inclination, an ephemeral poetic flower, which has no more consequence for the individual himself than for the human race." These eloquent lines were penned by Mr. Sabatier,* and it is hard to see how they fit in with the theory of salvation by faith independent of beliefs. A Catholic has a perfect right to conceive of the tradition "as the objective revelation of the interior life of the Church and of its piety, as something not in the least dead and immutable but a power which continues in ourselves."† Our theologians do not have ideas any different of ecclesiastical tradition considered in its act as

---

* *Op. cit.*, 405.
† *Op. cit.*, 406.

permanent organ of revelation. What they would not want to admit is that this "objective revelation" should be considered by the Christian individual as not having occurred, that it should be stripped of all authority in relation to him, that he should have the right to behave as if it did not exist, and only to retain what suited him. What will seem to them equally inconceivable is that this tradition of faith could exist, be maintained, and endure "independently of beliefs," that is to say, if the Christian is not in agreement, with respect to the faith and the economy of religion, with those who have lived before him and with those who now, like him, look to the faith for their salvation.

The theory of salvation by faith independently of beliefs is entirely new in the history of Christianity. What becomes of salvation and faith if the beliefs of which they are the objects are immaterial? One might just as well say one will be saved by faith without any belief whatever. This statement is clearly absurd, which is why one does not say it, but it is the logical equivalent of the first. Partisans of this point of view avoid proclaiming salvation by faith without belief; what they want to say is that salvation is not affected by the particular nature of the belief, that one will make whatever one can of the idea of God, of Christ, and even of salvation; that one will be saved as soon as one believes in some way or other that one is reconciled to God through Jesus. Each person is to be allowed to imagine God, Christ, and salvation as he thinks fit. One might make God the category of the ideal, Christ the type of man, and salvation the consciousness of duty: one would be saved because one had learned from Jesus to align one's will in harmony with the supreme law of the good. Other more concrete notions of religion would doubtless be ranged beside that one: they would have no better authority. But has one any longer the right to speak of God, of faith, of salvation, or should one not rather speak exclusively of man, of his ideal which corresponds to what men of old used to call God, of the concrete type of this ideal which corresponds to what men of old called God made man, of the realization of this type which corresponds to what men of old called salvation? Why not say that man is for himself his own God, his own Christ, and his own salvation?

We should beware of thinking it would be so easy to be saved thus. Rather, ask how many people would be capable of being so by this method? The good souls in Protestant temples who listen to the preaching of liberal pastors, persuaded that they belong, with them, to the Church of Christ, seek salvation in believing quite simply what they are taught according to the received creed. As for the teachers themselves, it is not for want of confidence in their own theories that they fail to profess them as dogma obligatory for all; it is because they are unable to deceive themselves in respect of the individual character of these theories, the impossibility of making them intelligible to the mass of believers, and getting them accepted by the elite of theologians without opposition. In order to spare themselves reciprocal anathemas, they declare that the elevated and purely individualistic way of salvation is the privilege of the few, a sort of personal possession belonging to each of those who follow it. Princes of thought, men of the spirit, they are outside the common laws; they remake religion for themselves, they re-create God, Christ, and salvation, not as objects of their system of worship and their hope, but as the forms of their very elevated conscience. They no longer journey in reality; they float on clouds of glory; they are the gods of the universe. No, it is not easy, and cannot but be dangerous to be saved in that way.

Faith reaches God, who is absolute, through the formulation of faith, which is contingent. But even though the relativity of formulations may be established in principle, this is still no reason to hold them to be immaterial. For formulations cannot be immaterial to the truth they express, nor to the religious society which employs them. It is undoubtedly true that one must not "mistake the historically and psychologically conditioned character of all doctrines or wish to rid the absolute of what has been born in time and must of necessity be modified in order to persist in time," an error which Mr. Sabatier* describes as that of "orthodoxy" in general, and which in fact belongs only to Protestant orthodoxy; but it is necessary to regulate the use of the formulations in harmony with the combined interests of the truths they have to express and the souls they help to instruct, as the Catholic Church does: should the whole of religious tradition also be abandoned without restraint to private judgment, as if each believer were its sovereign master and absolute arbiter, as if the individual who does not, in any other order, build himself up unaided, nor exist only for himself, were obliged, in the religious order, to see to his own education all by himself and exist for himself alone. Since religion is a social fact, since revelation is for everyone, since the religious life of the individual is nothing else than a communion in the divine life with other men, there must be common beliefs and common symbols through which each person can partake in the universal communion.

The relativity of traditional symbols dispenses no one from the obligation to receive them, for no one can avoid the necessity of using them; but it does mean that those appointed to teach in a believing society are

* Op. cit. 407.

bound always to explain them in the light of the times, so that those symbols do not become unintelligible and empty forms. Therefore, it will not be enough to repeat them in order to make them understood. It is only possible to resolve the contradiction which is or seems to be presented by the necessity of an absolute religious faith and the inevitable relativity of symbols, the individual character of faith and the community indispensable to belief, by means of an infallible Church, one that has full authority to regulate the symbols, explain them, adapt them to the variable conditions of society and the times. Otherwise nothing will be able to stop religion from petrifying into lifeless forms or to succumb to a complete anarchy of religious beliefs and society. It is tradition which teaches religion; it cannot teach it effectively except by bringing itself within the grasp of those to whom it speaks. It is tradition which guards religion; it cannot guard it if it has no authority, if it is not itself religious authority. A religion that ceases to be a Church, and a Church that abandons its authority no longer exist except in appearance.

"The psychological necessity for each believer to harmonize his personal religious conscience with the general culture he has acquired"* is not incompatible with respect for the tradition in which he lives and the authority which is its universal interpreter, whereas the premeditated and willful abandonment of tradition, even under the name of "critical symbolism," is merely a form of vulgar rationalism by which entirely personal conceptions are substituted for the age-old symbols of religious truth. It is impossible to renounce tradition without also placing oneself outside religion. The individual effort of religious thought is only valid and fruitful when it is voluntarily and in actual fact coordinated with the common effort which is carried on simultaneously in all living members of Christian society and which finds official expression in the teaching of the Church. The idea of a religion without any bond other than the freedom conceded to everyone to think what he likes in the order of religious things is not feasible, such freedom being capable only of scattering souls and not of uniting them. And if one admits that freedom is restricted by the fact that religious truth is one at its root, must it not also be recognized that the service of this unique truth has become more and more perfectly organized the better it has become known, through a permanent tradition which safeguards the truth in safeguarding itself, which gives everyone the benefit of all the experience of the past, which benefits from all the expe-

---

* *Op. cit.*, 409.

rience of the present? In the reality of history, no religion has ever existed without religious tradition; and it is certain that the Christian religion, wherever it exists, and even among the Protestants, is identified with Christian tradition. It will never be Christian individualism, because the principle of individualism is directly opposed to the very essence of religion and of Christianity.

New Theology

Charles Maignen
Translated by Christine E. Thirlway

On every point at once the traditional doctrine of the Church is being assailed; on every side Christian thought thwarted, Catholic meaning falsified.

Dogma, morals, discipline, the Holy Scriptures, tradition, philosophy, natural law, nothing can escape this influence whose pernicious activity insinuates itself everywhere.

The faith is in peril; the Church's divine constitution is threatened, and yet many stubbornly refuse to see the danger.

Will this licentious proliferation of errors one day give birth to some great heresy? There are grounds to fear it, for under all these variant forms of the spirit of novelty lies a common thought from which the others proceed, a master concept which gives force and cohesion to the whole.

Lamennaisianism,[1] Catholic Liberalism, Traditionalism, Rosminianism,[2] Catholic Socialism, Americanism,[3] et cetera, are no more than episodes in the intellectual and religious movement of our time. There is a system still vaster, still more capable of extending into and infiltrating all the sciences: it is Evolutionism. The incursion of this theory into the domain of theology is the greatest danger threatening the faith today.

Restricted at first to the natural sciences, it soon extended to history and then to religion. Anglo-Saxon in origin, it is admirably suited to the intellectual aptitudes of that race whose predominance, already so menacing in the domain of facts, it is therefore able to promote in that of ideas.

It is, therefore, an error of the future, an invasive and conquering idea, which deserves the most serious attention. We have already drawn attention to the audacity of a writer in the *Contemporary Review* who, under the pseudonym of "Romanus,"[4] has applied the Evolutionist theories to the dogmas and discipline of the Church. Today it is in France that we observe the incursion of the same ideas.

In the *Revue du Clergé Français* of December 1898, Father Loisy, under the pseudonym of A. Firmin, sets out the theory of what he calls *Le développement chrétien*. It is under the patronage of Cardinal Newman that this erstwhile professor at the Institut catholique de Paris presents the French public with the ideas of the new school of theology.

In 1845, Newman published a work entitled *An Essay on the Development of Christian Doctrine*. He was converted to Catholicism while writing this book.

It is what one calls nowadays a human document: the story of a soul in good faith gradually coming to a knowledge of the truth.

The very character of this book forbids one to seek in it anything other than Newman's personal reasons for becoming a Catholic, reasons which, according to the circumstances and particular dispositions of his mind, made the most decisive impression on him.

But to seek from the pen of a neophyte the fundaments of a new apologetic or of a system destined to renew theological studies, is both an imprudent venture and a very dangerous illusion.

Yet such is Father Loisy's idea, such the object of his study in the *Revue du Clergé Français*.

Here is how, under the aegis of the illustrious convert, he presents the basic principle of the whole system by which he thinks to explain the progress of dogma and the constitution of the Church:

"Newman's principal proposal is that an idea which is living, real, and nonabstract, which takes possession of men's minds, follows a line of development quite different from that taken by an axiom of geometry, the conclusions of which are deduced mathematically one from another. The fortunes of such an idea depend largely on the minds which have received it and labor on it further."

Here we are faced from the very first with an assertion which is, to say the least of it, singular. What is an "idea which is living, real, and nonabstract"?

All ideas are living and also real, but their reality is purely ideal, for they cannot exist outside the intellect. An axiom of geometry is an idea just as "real," just as "living," as the ideas of fatherland, family, or God. If this expression, "a living idea," is no more than a rhetorical figure, a metaphor, we may accept it as such, but it cannot have any further significance.

Yet this is what is claimed by the new school interpreted by Mr. Loisy.

For this school, the "living idea" is a subjective reality which "develops" in men's minds along a line "quite different" from that of abstract ideas: not, like these, by way of syllogism and according to the laws of logic, but by way of a sort of germination.

As a plant grows and develops by assimilating everything which can serve to nourish it in the place where it germinated, so it is with a "living idea" in the human mind.

"A relation becomes established between the idea and all the preoccupations of those who entertain it. It is as if it attracts into its orbit anything which is not contrary to it or with which it might have some positive affinity, and rejected everything not of its kind or in direct opposition. It grows by assimilating whatever surrounds it, and its purity comes not from isolating itself from everything, but from dominating everything, from perpetuating itself by dominating everything which approaches it. In consequence, the history of such an idea is that of a perpetual struggle, and the times of silence are not those in which the idea flourishes and grows. Whatever risk of corruption may attend contact with the world, this risk must be run if the truth is to be understood and receive fuller manifestation."

One already sees some of the practical consequences it will be easy to deduce from such a theory, if once what Mr. Loisy says about ideas should be applied to dogmas. But may one not wonder at the nonchalance with which such gratuitous assertions are aired in the full light of day and, in the absence of any attempt at demonstration, placed like a solid foundation at the base of a whole system claiming to reform philosophy and religion?

Every "living idea," sown in the human mind like a seed in a furrow, grows and develops there according to the principle of life within it and the homogeneous and assimilable elements it finds in the mind that carries it. The "living idea" will therefore be subject to transformation and change analogous to those that turn an acorn into an oak.

"Here below, to live is to change," says Mr. Loisy, "and to be perfect is to have changed often. Such is the law of all real development in humanity: such is also the law of religious development."

So there we have it.

"Religious development," "Christian development," is fulfilled according to the laws we have just described.

Dogma is a "living idea," and it is in this sense that the innovators understand the expression "the life of dogma" and busy themselves about making it part of the language of theology.

It is scarcely necessary to demonstrate how much this theory conflicts with traditional doctrine. This, Mr. Loisy does not contest, but he considers it permissible to defend this system as a scientific hypothesis, and adds that it alone is capable of satisfying the modern mind.

It is here that we come to the very crux of the issue between the modern mind and Catholic doctrine, and that we surprise yet another strategy devised in the hope of escaping the condemnations of the Vatican Council, recalled by Leo XIII in his letter to Cardinal Gibbons.[5]

In the following lines the system of "Christian development" is also revealed as the theological basis of Americanism.

"The preservation of dogmas *in eodem sensu eademque sententia* excludes from doctrinal development contradiction, the substitution of one meaning for another under the same form of words, *but not the interpretation of a traditional truth by means of notions connatural,* if one may be allowed so to express it, *to the first expression of those truths.* Since the end of the first century, what has Christian theology been if not a constant and ever-renewed effort to establish a sort of equation or perpetual correspondence between the interpretation of the revealed dogmas and the intellectual progress of humanity?"

We do not claim to have grasped the entire meaning of these somewhat obscure explanations, but what the author wants to say is plain enough.

The "first expression" of dogmatic truths was determined by the need to establish "a sort of equation" between the interpretation of revealed dogmas and the intellectual level at the time of their definition.

It is not therefore substituting a new for an old meaning to give a dogma an interpretation which will be "connatural" to the old interpretations, because it will give contemporary minds precisely the same satisfaction as the old interpretations gave the minds of the preceding generations.*

The "perpetual correspondence between the interpretation of revealed dogmas and the intellectual progress of humanity" is the great law which governs the science of theology in present, past, and future.

It is the idea clearly expressed on this page:

---

* According to modern exegetes, the same theory applies to the interpretation of texts of the Holy Scriptures.

"It is easy to understand that Christianity had to have a development...because it was a universal religion which could not help but be transformed, enriched, and enlarged by its operation in relation to the world in which it was called to live; because it was impossible, even on the most important points of doctrine, to hold to the letter of the Scriptures without falling into a vain worship of forms;...because in the Scriptures themselves revelation is subject to a progressive development and *there would seem to be no good reason why this development should suddenly have come to an abrupt end with the death of the last Apostle*; because the idea of a doctrine entirely perfect from the very beginning and having nothing to gain from subsequent investigations, applications, and experiences, is inconceivable and absurd."

The idea of a doctrine "entirely perfect from the beginning" is nonetheless the traditional idea the Church has always held of its doctrine. There is, undoubtedly, a certain progress within this doctrine, according to the celebrated prescription of Vincent de Lérins. But it is not the dogma which develops and is transformed, it is the human mind, assisted by grace, which penetrates more deeply into the knowledge of the faith.

Far from having been incomplete or generally veiled in mystery, the revelation of dogmas was perfect and transparent from the beginning. "*It is not the faith which progresses in the faithful*," says Albert the Great, "*but the faithful who progress in the faith*."

This is so true that such progress of the faithful in the faith, by means of the Church's definitions which set out more clearly and more explicitly what Christians of previous ages implicitly believed, such progress, we say, applies only to the mass of believers. For, in the case of the Saints and Doctors of the Church, it is certain that each of them, according to the lights he received from above, believed with an explicit and formal faith dogmas which were not defined by the Church until several centuries after them.

As for the apostles, pillars and foundations of the Church of God, the common teaching of the theologians is that they had an explicit belief in all the dogmas since defined by the Church and all those that may yet be proposed by the infallible magisterium until the end of time.

It is therefore not the dogma which develops and grows in the Church with the passage of time, it is the Church which proclaims down the centuries with ever more luminous clarity and increased force, the dogmas which heresy was determined to attack.

As long as a truth is not contested, it is enough for it to be believed implicitly by the mass of the faithful, while those to whom God gives more supernatural light believe it explicitly. But when heresy appears, the implicit faith of the masses is exposed to grave danger, it no longer offers them sufficient defense against the lures and wiles of error; then the Church fortifies with its anathemas the frontiers of the dogma under attack, demanding from everyone an explicit faith in the truth under siege.

Such is the traditional conception of the progress of faith in the Church.

The idea of a dogma in the form of a seed, planted in the world by Jesus Christ like a grain in the furrow, runs counter to the dogmatic facts and the most sure doctrines of Christianity.

It is impossible to understand how Father Loisy could have written, with reference to Newman:

"He saw, just as clearly as the Protestant scholars who have written recently on the subject of the history of Christian dogmas and the philosophy of religion, that when the Savior was put to death, the Apostles had neither a clearly defined organization nor a fixed creed nor a program of religious action or worship to institute."

Undoubtedly, at the moment of Our Savior's death, the apostles had not yet been confirmed in the faith, but was Pentecost an event of no significance to the history of dogma? And can one say that the apostles, when they started to preach the Gospel, had "neither a fixed creed, nor a program of religious action or worship to institute"?

It was not by way of assimilation and development that their minds were fully enlightened, it was by the sudden and perfect illumination of grace.

Up to the end of time the Church will continue to draw its illumination from the source of these divine rays.

"Up to the present, the Catholic Church has not reflected a great deal on her history, having always had better things to do; she has defined nothing, she has no positive teaching on the mode of her development."

Thus writes A. Firmin (Fr. Loisy) in the *Revue du Clergé Français*. Here we meet once again the endlessly repeated error of Liberal Catholicism and Americanism. Even if the Church has "defined" nothing on "the mode of her development," it does not at all follow that she "has no positive teaching" on this subject.

The traditional doctrine of the Fathers and the Doctors, the common and permanent sentiment of Catholic theologians constitute "a positive teaching" of the Church, which one is *obliged in conscience* to accept and to follow. This is what the Vatican Council said. If one separates oneself from the teaching of the ordinary magisterium of the Church, one may be able to do it without being a heretic but not without committing a mortal sin against the faith. That is what the "innovators," the "liberals," the "Americanists" seem constantly to forget.

The Catholic Church has a very positive teaching on "the mode of her development," and to claim that "up to the present [she] has not reflected a great deal on her history" is to fall short of the truth and of the respect due from a son to his mother.

We have briefly recalled a number of points of Catholic doctrine which cannot be reconciled with the theory of "Christian development" attributed to Newman by the *Revue du Clergé Français*; we shall continue this study whose practical applications will appear in every line.

For want of having reflected sufficiently on her history, the Catholic Church had therefore failed to understand, up to the present, the providential role of heresies. These not only present the Church with the opportunity to affirm her faith and to throw additional light on her dogma, it is by means of *assimilation* that dogma profits from error. Listen to Fr. Loisy:

"The power of assimilation…which guarantees to the Church in the form of a legitimate development *what heresy first worked out in an incomplete and irregular fashion*; thus the Montanists are seen to have foreshadowed religious asceticism, the Gnostics Christian theology, Sabellius Saint Augustine's Trinitarian concept."

So, the "progress of the faith," the "Christian development" are effected first, but in incomplete and irregular fashion, by heresy; the Church finishes and legitimizes this work by assimilating it to itself, as a plant assimilates the elements contained in the air and soil in which it lives.

This idea is formulated still more precisely when the author says:

Ecclesiastical theology is "the diligent and patient elaboration of a single doctrine from very varied materials, and the Catholic system of worship represents the sanctification by Christianity of rites which would otherwise be without any value and of which a number have been able to exist in other religions;…"

What a naturalist conception of the Church! More than that, filled with Evolutionist theories, the writer in the *Revue du Clergé Français* goes as far as to confuse under the same name and to compare as if they flowed from the same principle, the marvels accomplished in souls by God and the tricks perpetrated by Satan:

"Asceticism, which in other religions becomes the expression of a mindless fanaticism, in Catholicism holds its own as a discipline of genuine virtue and a universal service; mysticism, which elsewhere produces extravagances of doctrine and conduct, has formed great Saints in the Roman Church."

Is it not a painful spectacle to see the *Revue du Clergé Français* publish such doctrinal *enormities,* verging on blasphemy, without a unanimous protest being raised against such aberrations?

It comes as no surprise, at this juncture to find Mr. Loisy presenting Christianity as a kind of result of post-exilic Judaism and ancient philosophy.

"Christianity is in a very true sense a development from post-exilic Judaism, which is a development from the religion of the prophets, which is a development from primitive Mosaic Yahwism, which is a development from the religion of the patriarchs, which had its beginnings in the religion of prehistoric humanity."

This conception of "progress" and of the "life of dogma" down the ages is, we repeat, purely naturalistic. It would be understandable in the rationalist historian who reasons from outside appearances and does not understand the divine character of the successive revelations, but it is inexcusable for the Christian and the priest to speak in this way of the things of God.

It is not by way of successive development that God has communicated the truth to men. Suarez considers, in line with theological opinion, that Adam received a very complete knowledge of the mysteries of the Incarnation and the Redemption; the head of fallen humanity believed in his Redeemer with a more explicit faith than did his descendants, even those nearest to messianic times. In the same way Moses and David were certainly more enlightened than any of the sages or prophets of *pre- or postexilic* Judaism, the first on the subject of the ancient law and the mysteries it figured and the second in respect of the humiliations and the glory of Christ the King.

This is the common teaching of the theologians, a teaching founded on the Catholic tradition and a true understanding of the supernatural character of Revelation.

Divine revelation is neither an axiom from which the human reason necessarily and rigorously deduces the consequences, nor a seed which develops in the human mind by assimilating whatever is appropriate to its principle of life: it is a deposit which man receives by grace and preserves intact only with God's help.

Under the old covenant, when this deposit was at risk and the promise of the Messiah to come was in danger of vanishing from human memory, God intervened with physical prodigies, himself calling to mind and renewing his promise. Under the law of grace, Christ, ever-living in his Church, lends his continuous assistance to prevent the deposit of faith entrusted to the Apostles from being corrupted. But though there may be growth in the external defenses that protect dogma against the enemy, there is neither growth nor change in dogma itself.

According to the theory of "Christian development" and of the "life of dogma" the Church of the first three centuries of our era had as yet only an imperfect development, a "life" like that of an infant, in relation to the present-day Church and, so to say, *dogmas in embryo.*

Is it not obvious that good Christian sense must be repelled by this idea which, however, follows very logically and necessarily from the new theory?

Truly living dogmas are those for which one dies, and the humblest Christian will not hesitate to believe that in the catacombs Catholic dogma had an intensity of life it has not enjoyed in any other times, above all our own.

But one of the faults of our "innovators" is to muddle and confuse the most widely disparate notions; they do not distinguish the dogma either from its defense or from its scientific presentation, and because the Fathers of the Church spoke the language of their times and formulated the Christian truths using words which had already been used by pagans, they think it permissible to conclude that human science contributed to the deposit of revelation.

"Is it not true," says Fr. Loisy, "that the idea of the Logos, before its entry into the fourth Gospel, into the apologetics of the Fathers, and into Christian theology of the third century, was also a scientific theory? Is it not evident that the idea of consubstantiality, before being canonized at Nicea and the idea of transubstantiation, before being applied to the Eucharist, were purely scientific notions? Was not the idea of the native corruption of human nature, which Saint Augustine elaborated in his theory of grace, rooted as much in a philosophical doctrine as in the Scriptures?

"All these scientific theories may be said to have strengthened and even, historically speaking, saved traditional Christianity in their day."

Indeed, the philosophy of antiquity rendered signal service to the Church, but as a helper and as the handmaid of theology. The ideas of consubstantiality and transubstantiation may be analyzed and defined solely by means of a syllogism, but if faith had not taught men the mysterious facts which these ideas represent, philosophy would never have penetrated so far into the profundities of being.

To complete the account of this theology, truly new in the Church, it is not enough to show how dogmas are built up and develop, it must also be seen how the dead wood and parasitic growths which hinder their growth are excised.

Each new development, says Mr. Loisy, "produces a kind of wastage." This is a pretty term and deserves to be explained in the actual words used by its author:

"In appropriating and transforming for its own use the scientific notions that seemed best to express its thought and its life, the Church has discarded more than one inadequately formulated fragment of incomplete doctrine which tradition had previously carried without repugnance and sometimes even with a certain approval."

Thus the normal "development" of the "life of dogma" is necessarily accompanied by "a kind of wastage" that may even extend to doctrines and formulations which "tradition may up to then have carried without repugnance and sometimes even with a certain favor."

This view seems of a nature such as to cause some anxiety to timorous spirits, especially as the author takes the trouble to tell us that an exaggerated fear of this doctrinal "wastage" is the principal obstacle to true development.

"It should be noted that one of the most ordinary causes of corruption or false development in the religious order is the fixed determination not to follow the idea in its evolution and to enclose oneself blindly in the tradition of the past."

Up to the present the Church has always maintained that the love of novelty is the greatest obstacle to the integrity of the faith. The new theology has changed all that. It is attachment to the tradition of the past, "the fixed determination not to follow the idea in its evolution," which is "one of the most ordinary causes of *corruption* or false development in the religious order." Now, what are the limits, what are the laws for this evolution of the idea and, in consequence, of the dogma?

As long as *unity of type* be maintained, one must be ready to welcome an evolution or transformations "as considerable in their order as, in the physiological order, are those of animal life from its embryonic to its perfect state."

It is already a great deal—it is already a great deal too much—to compare the development of Catholic doctrine to the physiological transformations of a living being, but if one reflects that the same school more or less accepts Darwin's theories, one sees just how far this thesis might go!

It goes far indeed, this idea of the physiological development of dogmas.

Le Sillon of 25 May 1899 commented à propos of the article by Fr. Loisy at present under consideration:

"We may perhaps go even further. What does it matter after all that the Fathers sometimes sought the seed of certain dogmas in scriptural texts which in fact have quite a different meaning? These exegetical errors are not the source of the belief of Christian writers; but this belief flourished by way of an intimate germination on the vigorous trunk of revealed dogma and the Fathers, dominated by this idea, then discovered its primitive expression in texts of the Scriptures to which, in some cases, this belief was entirely alien.

"What does it matter even if Catholic dogma borrowed the elements of its development from the ideas of philosophy and may have been subjected to the influence of more or less erroneous beliefs current in Christian milieus at the time of its formation? God has arranged these alien influences so that they do not sully the purity of dogma, so that they even contribute to its development."

False interpretations of Scripture, the erroneous opinions of the common herd or the systems of the philosophers, these are what contribute to the development of dogmas and function as a sort of medium for the culture of the dogmatic microbe. Here we have, in a new guise, the theory of *providential errors* developed by Romanus in the *Contemporary Review*.

One is forced to conclude that all these are sister ideas, all these schools: Liberalism, Americanism, Evolutionism, hang together. We shall bring still more proofs.

One would, moreover, be loath to assert that the peculiar doctrines called in question above are personal to Father Loisy. More than a year after he had formulated them in this way, on 31 October 1900, *La Vie Catholique* published an article on Fr. Loisy which clearly indicates the bonds of solidarity uniting him to the Americanist and liberalist party. Here is the document!

"The *Revue du Clergé Français* has the great honor of publishing, from time to time, a long work signed with this name: *A. Firmin*. Approximately every three months, thirty or so pages appear on one or other aspect of exegesis or apologetics. We are proud to say that they are impatiently awaited by Catholic scholars all over the world, and that under this pseudonym everyone recognizes Father Loisy, doctor of theology, former professor at the Institut catholique de Paris.

"It was the diocese of Châlons which had the task of educating and instructing him. When one remembers that Mgr. Meignan was bishop of that city, one more readily understands the felicitous and extremely intellectual influence which directed his education. But for such men, analysis of the external circumstances in which they developed is not enough and fails to explain their power.

"It is almost immaterial for us to know that Mr. Loisy was a pupil at the Institut catholique before being a professor there; that he found in Mgr. d'Hulst a rector who was his friend and able to understand him; that, for a long time, in the little room where he lectured, he was able to teach a few disciples that exegesis, like all the other sciences, requires honesty and fidelity; that it was then that he devoted himself to creating and directing a review extremely highly regarded by the specialists, *Enseignement Biblique*, in which his lectures were published, and which today comprises the most formidable arsenal arrayed by Christian criticism against Renanist exegesis.

"In order to appreciate him it must above all be remembered how slowly he developed, in complete sincerity, little by little uncovering the route and unobtrusively extending it. It is also admirable and should be brought to the fore that he always knew how to defer to authority and, where necessary, to submit. For a long time he enjoyed the protection of this wonderful ivory tower in which he studied in silence. It was an article of popularization, inadequate though well-intentioned, which set on his heels a long succession of critics, startled to be told in a day all that he had been repeating for many years, who began to attack him furiously, not daring to take on the actual author of the article. . . .

"Following these events he left the Université catholique. He retired to Neuilly, where he became chaplain to the Dominicans. In this very pure environment one was able to taste the piety of this scholar. . . . But the way which seemed to have been made sweet and fresh for him led once again into the desert. His health, shaken by successive blows, deteriorated to a point where he was obliged to resign his position, one which had allowed him to continue his work without other burdens. In the 1899 vacation he retired to Bellevue, where he has suffered and worked, leading a modest life maintaining himself solely and entirely by these studies which have appeared in the *Revue du Clergé* or the *Revue d'Histoire et de Littérature Religieuse*, and which are an ornament to French Catholic exegesis.

"One is beginning to recognize this power, so easily belied by a frail and slender appearance denoting weakness and modesty. The face, extremely pale and white, seems at first sight lifeless and to merge almost to nothing in the shadow of an order or an association. It is a personality which seems to feel it a duty to efface itself. And yet, he is in the first rank of those who are increasing in stature, freeing themselves from all those accumulated stratifications which, through the mysterious passage of time, have come to overlie the origins, and which are such fertile ground for the naturalists and rationalists. In the brilliance glimpsed in the depths of his eyes, mostly veiled under eyelids heavy with fatigue, confronted by that very high forehead, very broad and very pure, with a splendor like that of marble, one comes at last to recognize the silent and solitary spirit to whom have come in admiration great bishops like Mgr. Ireland, Mgr. Spalding, and Mgr. Mignot, Benedictines—and this is the finest homage—scholars among the laity such as Baron von Hügel.

"At first sight, these words may seem surprising. One may believe that all these adjectives, deliberately collected together and set round this name, are simply there to embellish the portrait. But when one recalls that Fr. Loisy is at the present time without doubt the greatest exegete in Catholicism, at once the most courageous and yet the most submissive to the authority of the writer of the encyclical *Providentissimus Deus*, it will be possible to forget the perhaps somewhat violent ebullience of those blithe spirits gathered round him by the force of their admiration, and one will wish to remember only his large eyes and that splendid forehead, the faith and genius, the work which continues in spite of the suffering and which is of so much profit to religion."

The article you have just read dates from a fortnight after the letter in which His Eminence Cardinal Richard condemned an article by A. Firmin published on 15 October 1900 in the *Revue du Clergé Français* under the title *la Religion d'Israel.*

Since that time, Father Loisy has stopped writing in that journal, but he has published as a brochure the articles that have already appeared, and his friends have had printed by lithograph, for clandestine distribution, the article whose publication has just been prohibited.

The doctrines that we have analyzed in this chapter are not those of a single isolated person, but of a school or, better still, a party.

Notes

Introduction

1. From 1888, when he was appointed professor at the University of Berlin, until his retirement in 1921, Adolf von Harnack (1851–1930) was the acknowledged leader of liberal Protestant thought. His *Das Wesen des Christentums* (1900)—English translation, *What Is Christianity?*—provided the occasion for Loisy's critique in *L'Évangile et l'Église*. On Harnack, see G. Wayne Glick, *The Reality of Christianity: A Study of Adolf von Harnack as Historian and Theologian* (New York: Harper and Row, 1967).

2. For early reader reactions to *L'Évangile et l'Église*, see Émile Poulat, *Histoire, dogme et critique dans la crise moderniste* (Tournai: Casterman, 1979), 125–60.

3. Gabriel Daly, *Transcendence and Immanence* (Oxford: Clarendon Press, 1980).

4. Alfred Loisy, *The Gospel and the Church*, trans. Christopher Home (London: Isbister, 1903). Republished, with an introduction by Bernard B. Scott (Philadelphia: Fortress Press, 1976); with an introduction by R. Joseph Hoffman (Buffalo, N.Y.: Prometheus Books, 1988).

5. François Richard (1819–1908), bishop of Belley (1871–1875), coadjutor of the archdiocese of Paris (1875–86), succeeding as archbishop until his death. See Maurice Clément, *Vie de Cardinal Richard* (Paris: J. de Gigord, 1924).

6. Alfred Loisy, *The Religion of Israel*, trans. Arthur Galton (London: T. Fisher Unwin, 1910).

7. Charles Maignen (1858–1937) was an ardent polemicist against innovating currents in theology. He opposed Americanism with his *Le Père Hecker est-il un saint?* (1897), a critique he continued in *Nouveau catholicisme et nouveau clergé* (Paris: Victor Retaux, 1902). "Théologie nouvelle," translated here as "New Theology," is drawn from the latter work, which actually went on sale toward the end of 1901.

8. In *La Vérité française*, February 4 through 9, 1903; second series in March 2, 4, 6, 7, 12, 14, and 21, 1903. For discussion of Maignen's critique, see C. J. T. Talar, "Reading Loisy," *Literature & Theology* 5 (1991): 49–67.

9. In *La Vérité française*, October 24, 25, 28, 29, and 30, 1903; second series in November 11, 12, 13, 17, 23, 26, and December 28, 1903.

10. The account here will be highly selective, given the availability not only of translations of Loisy's autobiographical writings, but also of secondary work on his development in relation to modernism, e.g., Bernard B. Scott's introduction to *The Gospel and the Church*; Valentine Moran, "Loisy's Theological Development,"

Theological Studies 40 (1979): 411–52; C. J. T. Talar, "Innovation and Biblical Interpretation: Alfred Loisy and *La Question biblique*," in *Catholicism Contending with Modernity: Roman Catholic Modernism and Anti-modernism in Historical Context*, ed. Darrell Jodock (Cambridge: Cambridge University Press, 2000).

11. Ernest Renan (1823–92) lost his Catholic faith while a seminarian at Saint-Sulpice. His *Vie de Jésus* (1863) became a veritable best seller and generated a cottage industry of Catholic refutations. See David C. J. Lee, *Ernest Renan: In the Shadow of Faith* (London: Duckworth, 1996).

12. See Vytas V. Gaigalas, *Ernest Renan and His French Catholic Critics* (North Quincy, Mass.: Christopher Publishing House, 1972), chap. 5.

13. Maurice d'Hulst (1841–96) became rector of the Paris Institut catholique in 1881. A renowned preacher, spiritual director, and apologist in his day, his attempt to intervene in the "biblical question" was less successful. See Alfred Baudrillart, *Vie de Mgr d'Hulst*, 2 vols. (Paris: J. de Gigord, 1921); and Francesco Baretta, *Monseigneur d'Hulst et la science chrétienne* (Paris: Beauchesne, 1996).

14. Maurice d'Hulst, "M. Renan," *Le Correspondant* 169 (October 25, 1892): 193–227, citing 202.

15. Marie-Joseph Lagrange (1851–1938), founder of the École biblique in Jerusalem (1890) and its *Revue biblique* (in 1892). More moderate in his use of historical criticism than Loisy, Lagrange nonetheless attracted suspicion, opposition, and occasional sanction from Catholics who felt threatened by a departure from a concentration on the dogmatic meaning of scripture.

16. See Bernard Montagnes, *Le Père Lagrange (1855–1938)* (Paris: Cerf, 1995); English translation, *The Story of Father Marie-Joseph Lagrange: Founder of Modern Catholic Biblical Study*, trans. Benedict Viviano (New York: Paulist Press, 2006), chap. 5. Lagrange's *La méthode historique* was translated as *Historical Criticism and the Old Testament* (London: Catholic Truth Society, 1906).

17. In addition to *L'Évangile et l'Église* and *Autour d'un petit livre*, the decree named *La religion d'Israël*, *Études évangéliques*, and *Le Quatrième évangile*. See *La Censure d'Alfred Loisy (1903)*, ed. Claus Arnold and Giacomo Losito (Rome: Liberia Editrice Vaticana, 2009).

18. The literature is ably summarized and evaluated by Ronald Burke, "Loisy's Faith: Landshift in Catholic Thought," *Journal of Religion* 60 (1980): 138–64.

19. For an account of Loisy's progress toward priesthood, see his *Choses passées* (Paris: Émile Nourry, 1913), 1–51. This has been translated into English as *My Duel with the Vatican*, trans. Richard Wilson Boynton (New York: Dutton, 1923; repr., New York, N. Y.: Greenwood Press, 1968). Loisy enlarged upon the material in *Choses passées* in his three-volume *Mémoires pour servir à l'histoire religieuse de notre temps* (Paris: Émile Nourry, 1930–31). Volume 1, pp. 9–65, covers the period sketched here. In his *Un séminaire français au 19ème siècle* (Paris: Téqui, 1977), Christian Dumoulin gives a portrait vif a provincial seminary (Bourges) very like the one Loisy experienced. For an appreciation of the manual tradition and the neo-scholasticism that constituted the regnant theology, see Daly, *Transcendence and Immanence*, chap. 1.

20. By 1880 the anticlerical parties had gained sufficient power to deprive the Catholic universities of both title- and degree-granting rights. They were rechristened *instituts catholiques*.

21. Louis Duchesne had studied in the secular university, where he had been exposed to more critical approaches to history than were inculcated in seminary. But he appears to have made little impact on Loisy at this point. See Loisy, *Mémoires*, 1:74.

22. Ibid., 80.

23. Ibid., 81—including, of course, the Firmin articles.

24. Louis Duchesne's critical approach to church history caused him difficulties during his tenure as faculty member at the Paris Institut catholique. In 1895 he was named director of the École française de Rome, a post he occupied until his death. See Brigitte Waché, *Monseigneur Louis Duchesne (1843–1922)* (Rome: École française de Rome, 1992).

25. Loisy has left descriptions of Renan's procedure in *Choses passées*, 64–65 (*My Duel with the Vatican*, 92–93), and in "Le cours de Renan au Collège de France," *Journal de psychologie normale et pathologique* 20 (1927): 325–30.

26. That of Constantin Chauvin, *Leçons d'introduction générale aux divines écritures* (Paris: P. Lethielleux, 1898), is representative in providing exegetical rules with illustrations and applications.

27. Loisy, *Choses passées*, 54–56, 64, 83ff (*My Duel with the Vatican*, 85–86, 92, 106ff.).

28. Loisy's lectures for 1889–90 were published as *Histoire du canon de l'Ancien Testament* (Paris: Letouzey, 1890) and for 1890–91 as *Histoire du canon de Nouveau Testament* (Paris: Maisonneuve, 1891). In 1892 he began publishing his lectures in a little periodical he established, *L'Enseignement biblique*. A detailed bibliography of Loisy's extensive publications is provided in Émile Poulat, *Alfred Loisy, sa vie son oeuvre* (Paris: Éditions de Centre Nationale de la Recherche Scientifique, 1960), 303–24.

29. Poulat, *Histoire, dogme et critique dans la crise moderniste*, 8.

30. Loisy, *Choses passées*, 84–92 (*My Duel with the Vatican*, 107–13); Loisy, *Mémoires*, 1:172–79.

31. In 1885 Loisy made another attempt at reconciling Catholic tradition and scientific progress, but he judged the concessions exacted from the traditional dogmas unsustainable and gave up the enterprise. This manuscript no longer exists. See Loisy, *Mémoires*, 1:148–49.

32. Loisy describes these events in *Choses passées*, 124–46 (*My Duel with the Vatican*, 137–54), and in *Mémoires*, vol. 1, chaps. 8–9. More sympathetic to d'Hulst is Alfred Baudrillart, *Vie de Mgr d'Hulst*, 2 vols. (Paris: J. de Gigord, 1928), vol. 1, pp. 480–92, and vol. 2, chap. 21. For critical analysis, see Francesco Baretta, "La doctrine romaine de l'inspiration de Léon XIII à Benoît XV (1893–1920): La production d'une nouvelle orthodoxie," in *Alfred Loisy cent ans après "Autour d'un petit livre,"* ed. François Laplanche et al. (Turnhout: Brepols, 2007), 47–60.

33. Loisy, *Mémoires*, 1:261. Loisy goes on to detail these effects, quoting from his article. Originally published in *L'Enseignement biblique*, the complete text of

"La question biblique et l'inspiration des écritures" is accessible in Alfred Loisy, *Études bibliques* (Paris: Alphonse Picard, 1902), 170.

34. The *Essais d'histoire et de critique religieuses*, exists in manuscript form at the Bibliotheque nationale (Papiers Loisy I, Na Fr 15364, 126p.). Loisy judged the manuscript, completed in January 1898, as "very insufficient" and reworked it as *Essais d'histoire et de philosophie religieuses*, completing it in May 1899 (Papiers Loisy II, NR Fr 15635, 163p.). A typescript version of the latter, with notes by Louis Canet (1883–1958), comprises volumes 3 through 5 of the Papiers Loisy (Na Fr 15636–15638, 1134p.).

35. See Loisy, *Mémoires*, 1:442–77. The last chapter of the final section, "Le passé et l'avenir," has been published by Normand Provencher, "Un inédit d'Alfred Loisy," *Église et Théologie* 4 (1973): 391–413.

36. C. J. T. Talar, *Metaphor and Modernist: Alfred Loisy and His Neo-Thomist Critics* (Lanham, Md.: University Press of America, 1987).

37. Alfred Loisy, *L'Évangile et l'Église* (Paris: Alphonse Picard, 1902), 161–62 (*The Gospel and the Church*, 213–14).

38. Newman's *Essay on the Development of Christian Doctrine* is analyzed in Nicholas Lash, *Newman on Development* (Shepherdstown, W.Va.: Patmos Press, 1975). Chapter 7 treats the *Essay*'s impact on twentieth-century theology. For French reception of the *Essay*, see C. J. T. Talar, "Receiving Newman's *Development of Christian Doctrine*," in *Discourse and Context*, ed. Gerard Magill (Carbondale: Southern Illinois University Press, 1993), 167–80. On Loisy's relation to Newman, see Ronald Burke, "Was Loisy Newman's Modern Disciple?" in *Newman and the Modernists*, ed. Mary Jo Weaver (Lanham, Md.: University Press of America, 1985), 139–57.

39. Analyses of this first of the Firmin articles appear in William J. Wernz, "The 'Modernist' Writings of Alfred Loisy: An Analysis" (Ph.D. diss., University of Iowa, 1971), 68–75; and in Nicholas Lash, "Newman and 'A. Firmin,'" in *John Henry Newman and Modernism*, ed. Arthur H. Jenkins (Sigmaringendorf, Germany: Regio Verlag Glock und Lutz, 1990), 56–73. Francesco Turvasi, "The Development of Doctrine in John Cardinal Newman and Alfred Loisy," in *John Henry Newman, Theology and Reform*, ed. Michael E. Allsopp and Ronald R. Burke (New York: Garland, 1992), 145–87, concentrates primarily on *L'Évangile et l'Église* and *Autour d'un petit livre*.

40. Numbers in parentheses refer to the translation of the article under discussion.

41. For example, the statement of J.-B. Aubry regarding the function of exegesis is both representative and indicative: "The program of every professor of Sacred Scripture must be rigorously that of St. Thomas: *the investigation of the dogmatic meaning*—nothing else! Once this meaning is grasped, he possesses everything, for dogma is the germ of all that is good, above all of the mystical life." J.-B. Aubry, *Essai sur la méthode des études eccélesiastiques en France* vol. 2 (Lille: Desclée De Brouwer, n.d.), 382.

42. Wernz, "The 'Modernist' Writings of Alfred Loisy," 69.

43. Auguste Sabatier (1839–1901). As member, then dean, of the Protestant Theological Faculty at Paris, Sabatier advanced liberal Protestant theology in France. His *Esquisse d'une philosophie de la religion d'après la psychologie et l'histoire* (Paris: Fischbacher, 1897) developed ideas expressed earlier in *De la vie intime des dogmes et de leur puissance d'évolution* (Paris: Fischbacher, 1890). See Bernard Reymond, *Auguste Sabatier et le procès théologique de l'autorité* (Lausanne: l'Age d'homme, 1976), 37–39.

44. Loisy, *Mémoires*, 1:438. B. M. G. Reardon has argued that Loisy's evolutionary view of development in reality owed far more to Harnack and Sabatier than it did to Newman. B. M. G. Reardon, *Liberalism and Tradition: Aspects of Catholic Thought in Nineteenth Century France* (Cambridge: Cambridge University Press, 1975), 265.

45. Thomas Silkstone, *Religion, Symbolism and Meaning* (Oxford: Cassirer, 1968), appendix A: "The meaning of the word 'sentiment' in Sabatier's works," 142–47, citing 145.

46. Loisy, *L'Évangile et l'Église*, 170 (*The Gospel and the Church*, 220).

47. Stephen Sykes, *The Identity of Christianity* (London: SPCK, 1984), chap. 6, contains a particularly good discussion of these issues. See especially 132, 138–39.

48. On the increasingly moral emphasis Loisy came to place on Christianity, see *Choses passées*.

49. See Normand Provencher, *La révélation et son développement dans l'Église selon Alfred Loisy* (Ottawa: n.p., 1972), 36–41.

50. Avery Dulles, *Models of Revelation* (Garden City, N.Y.: Doubleday, 1983), 42. See also Werner Bulst, *Revelation* trans. Bruce Vawter (New York: Sheed and Ward, 1965).

51. Dulles, *Models of Revelation*, 44.

52. Ibid., 42.

53. Wernz, "The 'Modernist' Writings of Alfred Loisy," 88.

54. See Wendell S. Dietrich, "Loisy and the Liberal Protestants," *Sciences religieuses/Studies in Religion* 14 (1985): 303–11.

55. In his discussion of miracles Loisy sees his position as representative of a larger shift in Catholic thought. He is able to name Blondel as arriving at similar conclusions from a more philosophical perspective. At this point Loisy saw a solidarity between his work in exegesis and Blondel's in philosophy. See François Rodé, *Le miracle dans la crise moderniste* (Paris: Beauchesne, 1965).

56. Dermot Lane, *The Experience of God* (New York: Paulist Press, 2003), 26.

57. M. D. Petre, *Alfred Loisy: His Religious Significance* (Cambridge: Cambridge University Press, 1944), 112. Most closely associated with George Tyrrell, Maude D. Petre (1863–1942) knew many of the principal figures involved in the modernist crisis and herself came under ecclesiastical sanction. In addition to her autobiography, *My Way of Faith* (London: J. M. Dent and Sons, 1937), see Ellen Leonard, *Unresting Transformation: The Theology and Spirituality of Maude Petre* (Lanham, Md.: University Press of America, 1991).

The Development of Christianity According to Cardinal Newman

1. In October 1896, Loisy wrote to Friedrich von Hügel in response to some recommendations the baron had made regarding useful authors and their works. Specifically, he requested from von Hügel Newman's *Grammar of Assent, Idea of a University, An Essay on the Development of Christian Doctrine, Via Media* vol. 1, *Anglican Difficulties* 2, *Essays Critical and Historical,* and *University Sermons.* Alfred Loisy, *Mémoires pour servir à l'histoire religieuse de notre temps,* 3 vols. (Paris: Émile Nourry, 1930–31), 1:415.

2. Adolf von Harnack (1851–1930) used his vast historical erudition to compose his multivolume *Lehrbuch der Dogmengeschichte* (1886–89). [English translation, *History of Dogma* in 4 vols., trans. Neil Buchanan (New York: Dover, 1961).]

New Theology

1. Lamennaisianism derives its name from Félicité Lamennais (1782–1854), a pioneer of Catholic liberalism who advocated that the Church abandon its privileged place in civil society, and accept, at least *de facto,* the liberal notion of the state instead of the traditional Catholic one. The encyclicals *Mirari vos* (August 15, 1832) and *Singulari nos* (July 15, 1834) condemned his views.

2. Rosminianism: Antonio Rosmini-Serbati (1797–1855) was a prolific writer whose work touched upon many areas of philosophy and theology. Two of his works were placed on the Index in 1854; in 1887, under the pontificate of Leo XIII, forty propositions were extracted from his works and condemned. Supporters of Rosmini have denied that the censured propositions expressed Rosmini's true thought, a position officially accepted by the Church's magisterium in 2001.

3. Americanism refers to doctrines censured in Leo XIII's apostolic letter *Testem benevolentiae* (January 22, 1899). In addition to rejecting, as a general principle, that the Church should modify its doctrines in light of modern civilization, the letter targeted several specific errors, including an emphasis on natural virtues over supernatural virtues, a preference for active over passive virtues, the incompatibility of religious vows with modern freedom, and the adoption of a new apologetics. "Americanism" was really defined by French ultraconservatives, in controversies in which Charles Maignen played a pivotal role.

4. "Liberal Catholicism," *The Contemporary Review* (December 1897).

5. The reference is to *Testem benevolentiae.*

Index

Albert the Great, 91
Americanism, 87, 90, 92, 97, 106n.3
Anglicanism, 3, 8
animism, 20, 22
apologetics, vii, viii, xii–xiii, xvi, xviii,
    xxi, xxii, 13, 55, 64, 67, 74–76,
    79–80, 95
Aquinas, Thomas, ix, 56, 57n.
Arian controversy, 7
Aristotle, 7
Arius, 25
asceticism, 6, 7, 25, 94
Augustine, Saint, 6, 13
authority, xxi, 6, 8, 10, 14, 26, 38, 63,
    72, 83, 85
Autour d'un petit livre, viii, ix, xix, xxii

biblical question, xii, 10
Blondel, Maurice, 64–65, 66
Bossuet, Jacques-Benigne, xxii

Catholic Liberalism, 87, 92, 97
Choses passées, ix
Collège de France, viii, xi
conscience, 6, 19, 20, 21, 26, 31,
    42–44, 82
Contemporary Review, 97
Copernicus, 26
criteria of doctrinal development
  chronic continuance, 5, 7
  continuity of principles, xviii,
    4–5
  early anticipation, 5, 7, 11
  logical sequence, 5, 7
  power of assimilation, 5, 6
  preservation of the fundamental
    idea, xviii, 4
  preservative additions, 5
  unity of type, 4, 6, 96

Daly, Gabriel, vii
development, xii, xv, xvi, xviii, 26, 67,
    74, 79
  of doctrine/dogma, xiv, xxiii, 3–16,
    87–99
  See also criteria of doctrinal
    development
d'Hulst, Maurice, viii, xii, 98, 102n.13
doctrine, xii, xx, 34, 36, 47–48, 57,
    61–62, 63
  and revelation, 45
  and truth, 46
dogma, xiii, xvii–xviii, xx, xxi, xxiii,
    20, 22, 24–28, 36, 46–48, 50,
    59n., 78
Duchesne, Louis, x, 103nn.21, 24
Dulles, Avery, xx

École pratique des hautes études, x, xi
Enseignement biblique, 98
Essais d'histoire et de philosophie religieuse,
    xii, xv, xvi, xviii, xxi
Essay on the Development of Doctrine, An, xv,
    3, 12, 16, 88
Esquisse d'une philosophie de la religion, xx
essence of Christianity, xvii
essence of religion, 86
Évangile et l'Église, L', vii, viii, xii, xiv, xv,
    xvii, xviii, xix, xxii, xxiii
evolutionary naturalism, xxii

faith, xviii, xxiii, 17, 28, 43, 44, 47, 48, 57,
    60, 74, 76–80, 84–85, 91, 92, 96
  and miracles, 64, 68
  and reason, 6, 50
  salvation by faith, 26, 29, 83
false development, 4
Firmin articles, viii, xii, xiii, xv, xvi, xvii,
    xxi, xxiii

Galileo, 11, 26
Gibbons, James, 90
Gnostics, 6, 93
Grammar of Assent, 3
Gregory of Nyssa, 55

Harnack, Adolf, vii, xvi, xviii, 16, 17,
     18, 25, 31, 101n.1
heresy, 4, 6, 87, 93
historical Jesus, 21
Holy Spirit, 15, 47, 57n, 66, 79n
Hügel, Baron Friedrich von, 99,
     106n.1

Ignatius of Antioch, 7
individualist Christianity, xv, 23, 29, 32
Ireland, John, 99

Jesus Christ, 7, 8, 17, 18, 19, 20, 29,
     31, 50, 66, 67, 71, 72, 80, 83, 84,
     92, 94, 95
Judaism, 9, 23, 47, 94

Lacordaire, Henri, xi
Lagrange, Marie-Joseph, ix, 101n.15
Lamennaisianism, 87, 106n.1
Lane, Dermot, xxi–xxii
Leo XIII, 90, 106n.2
Loisy, Alfred, vii–xxiii, 88–99
Luther, 18, 23, 26

Maignen, Charles, viii, xxii, xxiii,
     101n.7, 106n.3
Maistre, Joseph de, 11
Marian devotion, 7
Meignan, Guillaume-René, 98
Méthode historique, La, ix
Mignot, Eudoxe-Irénée, 99
miracles, xiii, xxi, 17, 63–69, 73–74,
     80
modernism, vii, xiii
Möhler, Johann Adam, 11, 12
monolatry, 22
monotheism, 20, 22, 34, 46
Montalembert, Charles de, xi
Montanists, 6, 93
morality, 28, 34, 35, 40, 41, 57
mysticism, 7

natural religion, 6
neo-scholasticism, vii, xx
Newman, John Henry, xii, xvii
     and development of doctrine, xiv–xv,
          xviii, 3–16, 59 n, 77, 88, 92
Newton, Isaac, 11
Nicea, 13

Origen, 25

pantheism, 21
papacy, 6, 24
Pascendi dominici gregis, xxii
Petre, Maude, xxii
Pliny the Younger, 6
polytheism, 20, 22
positivism, 74
prayer, 7, 33, 53
prophecy, 63, 66–67, 69–75
Protestantism, 8, 18, 19, 29, 33, 45, 82
     Anglican, 8
     liberal, xvi–xvii, xviii, xxii
providence, 50, 65, 68, 70
Providentissimus Deus, 99

rationalism, xvi, xvii, xviii, xix, 17, 67,
     85
reason, 7, 37, 41, 49, 57, 68, 69
     and faith, 6, 50, 74–79
religion, xvii, xviii, xxi, 45, 46–47,
     49–62, 63, 67, 73–85
     definition of, 31–44, 45
     essence of, 24, 31
     individualist theory of, 17–29
Religion d'Israël, La, viii, 99
Renan, Ernest, viii, x, xii, 52, 54, 58,
     60, 62, 67, 102n.11
revelation, xiii, xv, xviii–xx, 17, 81–84,
     94
     and authority, 6
     and development, 5, 10
     economy of, 53
     idea of, 45–62
     proofs of, 63–80
     propositional theory of, xx, xxiii
     and religion, 31–32
Revue d'histoire et de littérature religieuses, 98
Revue du clergé français, vii, xii, xiii

Richard, François, vii, 99, 101n.5
Rosminianism, 87, 106n.2

Sabatier, Auguste, xix–xxi, 41, 82, 84,
        105n.43
    definition of religion, 32, 36, 39, 63
    and dogma, xviii
    and miracles, 64, 66, 68–69
    and prophecies, 70, 73
    as representative of liberal
        Protestantism, xii, xvi, xxii
    and revelation, 45, 56, 62, 65
    theory of religion, xvii, 17–29
Sabellius, 6, 93
Schleiermacher, Friederich, xvii
science, xix, 13, 17, 18, 22, 34–35, 43–44,
        57, 65, 67, 68–69, 74, 76, 81
Silkstone, Thomas, xvii
Sillon, Le, 97
Spaulding, John Lancaster, 99
Strauss, David Friedrich, 94
subordinationism, 7
Suetonius, 6

Tacitus, 6
Testem benevolentiae, 106nn.3, 5

tradition, 11, 18, 21, 28, 37, 38, 70, 82,
        85, 86
    Catholic, 8, 12, 13, 63
    Christian, 14, 71
    dogmatic, 17
    Roman, 8
traditionalism, 55, 87
truth, xiii, 4, 12, 28, 34, 35, 40–42,
        44, 46, 52, 54, 63, 81, 82,
        92, 94
    and apologetics, 74–76
    divine truth, 27, 51
    Scholastic definition of, 58

Vatican Council, xii, xiv, 25, 66, 67,
        90, 92
Vie catholique, La, 97
Vigouroux, Fulcran, xi
Vincent of Lérins, xiv, 11, 91
visions, 56, 57
Voltaire, 17

worship, 6, 7, 9, 25, 32, 92
    spirit worship, 38
    system of worship, 8, 10, 15, 34, 36,
        84